DALE EUNSON

UP ON THE RIM

Montana Historical Society
& Riverbend Publishing

Copyright © 1970, by Dale Eunson

Original elements of this edition copyright © 2002 by Riverbend Publishing.

Published by Riverbend Publishing, Helena, Montana in cooperation with the Montana Historical Society Press

Printed in Canada.

1 2 3 4 5 6 7 8 9 0 TP 07 06 05 04 03 02

All rights reserved. No part of this book may be reproduced, stored, or transmitted in any form or by any means without the prior permission of the publisher, except for brief excerpts for reviews.

Cover design by DD Dowden.
Text design by Suzan Glosser.

ISBN 1-931832-20-X

Cataloging-in-Publication data is on file at the Library of Congress.

RIVERBEND PUBLISHING
PO BOX 5833
HELENA, MT 59604

Toll-free 1-866-RVR-BEND
Fax 1-406-449-0330
www.riverbendpublishing.com

FOR
Dale Marie Weatherly
AND
John Kirby Weatherly

Introduction to Western History Classics

The idea behind Western History Classics is a simple one: to bring back into print books about Montana and the West that we believe deserve a second look. Some of these titles are much-loved classics for which we have received multiple requests to reprint over the years. Others are "lost classics," rescued from obscurity because we believe they still have much to offer modern-day readers. All have been selected with great care for their readability and power to illuminate some aspect of the region's rich literary and cultural heritage.

A special partnership between Riverbend Publishing, a Helena, Montana, commercial press, and the nonprofit Montana Historical Society Press has made this reprint series possible. Although both presses publish a variety of types of books under their own imprints, both share a commitment to rescuing Montana stories. It is out of this joint commitment that this series was born.

The subjects of the books in this series range widely across time and place to capture a rich variety of western experiences: from the natural wonders of the national parks to the artificial confines of Indian reservations, from thriving mining towns high in the Rocky Mountains to isolated homesteads on vast prairie expanses. Scholars specializing in Montana history and literature have recommended reprinting the titles included in this series, but that does not mean that all information in these books is accurate or that these reprints reflect the latest historiographical interpretations. Rather, these books offer particular, and sometimes quirky, points of purchase from which to view Montana's historical landscape. We expect readers will find some surprises within these volumes, which include both exemplary tellings of well-known stories and fresh perspectives that challenge commonly held notions about the West. Certainly, we hope they will come away with a new appreciation for the western experience in all its diversity. Happy reading.

Martha Kohl
Editor, Montana Historical Society Press

CONTENTS

1	"A Piano on a Dryland Farm in Montana?"	7
2	"It's Built Just Like My Squaw."	17
3	"It Will Be Fine and Dandy When We Get it Fixed Up."	27
4	"I Wouldn't Give Oleomargarine to a Dog!"	32
5	"There Goes Vesuvius!"	37
6	"Praise God From Whom All Blessings Flow."	47
7	"He won't take a gun to us, will he?"	56
8	"You Got to Hand It to That Guinea."	64
9	"I'll Pepper Your Tail with Buckshot!"	71
10	"Seems Like It's a Million Miles from Nowhere."	77
11	"Stallions That Danced on Golden Hooves."	87
12	"Nobody Could Hear Anything but the Hail."	98
13	"I'd Be a Millionaire Today If I Hadn't Been Such a Damn Fool."	109
14	"I Need a School Like I Need Smallpox!"	116
15	"And Just What Might Cow Chips Be?"	123

16	"When Your Time Comes, You Better Be Packed and Ready."	130
17	"Dogs Are Very Sensitive Creatures."	139
18	"Jim, Be Sure to Show Fern Your Bearskin."	149
19	"Shep Told Me."	158
20	"Are You Gentlemen in the Market for a Ford?"	167
21	"If It Gets Too Rough, Come and Talk to Me."	178
22	"Some Choose Not to Hear."	190
23	"Cross Your Heart and Hope to Die."	198
24	"Shake Hands with Bacon."	205
25	"Tell Him My Time Has Come."	217
26	"All at Once I knew What a Watch-eye Meant."	229
27	"But That's Papa's Name!"	235

FOREWORD

When I was a small boy, my family filed a claim on a homestead on the dry land of Montana. It was four miles northeast of Acton—up on the rim, as we called it. Being up there somehow gave us a certain cachet over the settlers on the flats to the west. That, we thought, was fit only for prairie dogs and sheepherders.

We lived there from 1910 to 1915, trying to scratch a living out of the wild and wonderful land that asked—and gave—no favor. We were hailed out, dried out, washed out, and blown out, yet my life was enriched and rewarded beyond measure by the experience.

This is the way I remember the first two years, but it all happened a long while ago, and time may have played tricks on me. All the people are real, and it all happened to them and to us, but I have changed the names of a few, because perhaps they remember it differently. My truth may not be their truth. If it is not, I beg their indulgence.

I owe a debt I can never repay to our old neighbors the Gullards—to Harry and Gladys, Carl and Mamie, and Selma Sharpe, and to Earl and Manda Hickson—all of whom helped me to remember the way it was when we were very young. And to Willard E. Fraser, former mayor of Billings, a neighbor I never met, who offered his assistance in typical Montana fashion.

"Montana," he wrote me, "is boy country, and sad the boy who doesn't have a chance to enjoy it."

I agree with him.

DALE EUNSON

INTRODUCTION

"Robert, what in heaven's name have you got there?"

Mamma's voice sounds far off, but that is just because I am not awake yet.

"Sssh. The kid still asleep?" That's Papa, whispering, not wanting to wake me up. Mamma doesn't answer out loud, but I can imagine her taking a look and shaking her head. Then she asks, "Where did you get him?" and Papa answers, "I bought him offen an old Indian for a dollar."

And I am thinking, where are we? Why aren't there any sheets on the bed? Why is the blanket so heavy? What's that funny smell? And what did Papa buy offen an old Indian for a dollar? I could open my eyes and find out, but that wouldn't be fair because I can tell by his voice that Papa wants to surprise me.

Then it comes to me where we are. Billings, Montana. We got here last night and slept at the livery stable. That's the smell: horses.

And then something bounds on the bed. I open my eyes and there is a collie pup licking my cold face with his warm, scratchy tongue. He is fat and black all over, except for brown dots over his eyes. One ear flops like a tiny mitten.

But it is not at his ear that I am staring. It is his right eye. It is cold and opal blue, while the other is brown and warm as velvet. I better not mention this, because maybe Papa and Mamma haven't noticed. If I point out that he's blind in one eye, Papa may take him back to the old Indian. But I guess I haven't fooled Papa.

"Don't fret about his eye," he says. "It's a watch."

"A what?" I say.

"A watch-eye. Damned if I know why they call 'em that."

"Robert, please," Mamma says. "Not every other word a cuss word. Dale is going to pick that up and give it right back to you in spades one of these days."

"Hell," Papa says, "I was just explaining about watch eyes. Some dogs are born with 'em. It don't interfere with their sight none."

"What's his name?" I want to know.

"Well," Papa says, "collies are s'posed to be shepherds. That's what we'll need him for. How about Shep?"

That sounds fine to me.

"Maybe you should have got a grown dog," Mamma is saying.

"Maybe," Papa says, "but..."

"You wouldn't take him back!" I yell.

"No," Papa says. "The Indian run as soon as he got shut

of him. I was just going to say—a grown dog might be more help to us right at the start, but old dogs sometimes take off and return to their old homes. This one, he'll grow up with us and be our dog from the word Go."

"Don't make me laugh," Mamma laughs. "Look at that, will you?"

Shep is sitting on my chest, tugging at one of my furlined mittens. It is so cold in the office of the livery stable where we spent the night that I still have on my mittens, mackinaw, and stocking cap.

"Hey, you, Shep, you leggo my mittens or I'll smack you!" Shep does not let go, and I do not smack him. He is already my dog, and I am his boy.

it for ten dollars an acre (which would amount to sixteen hundred dollars and nothing to be sneezed at) or hang on and farm it.

"It won't commit you to go out and take a look," Mamma said.

So Papa, whose term as sheriff was about to expire, decided to take a look. It was while he was out there the first time that he got to thinking about the reasons behind Mamma's itch to go West.

It was not so much that she wanted to live on a homestead, he told me when I was old enough to understand, as that she wanted to shake off the dust of Neillsville where his old friends could not seem to warm up to her or she to them. Mamma was his second wife. My mother had died of typhoid when I was fifteen months old and for three years after that he had tried to make do with the help of neighbors, an occasional housekeeper, and my pretty sister, Genevieve, who was just entering her teens and, of course, wanting to lead a full life of her own without being tied down to a baby brother.

I suspect I was really responsible for Papa's marriage to the town milliner. I had been running the streets of Neillsville—there were two automobiles in town at the time, a Kissel and a Stevens-Duryea, so the only hazard from traffic was an occasional runaway horse—and one of my stops had come to be the millinery shop. I used to hide in the enormous hat boxes of the period and leap out with an Indian war whoop to scare the daylights out of the customers, the good ladies of the town who were trying on the giddy Merry Widow hats.

Jessie Romaine, who owned the millinery establishment, was soft and warm and motherly. It was only natural that she would be concerned about a motherless child. She found me one night, alone, down by the depot, and took me home—to the jail. The sheriff thanked her, and within a few months they were married.

Papa was fifty-two at the time, and Jessie Romaine a thirty-three-year-old spinster who had come to Neillsville only a year before to set up shop. Perhaps there were other eligible ladies who had set their caps for the good-looking widower with two children—after his commendable period of mourning was over, of course. Or perhaps a milliner was suspect merely because she was a milliner. Milliners were always talked about in small towns. People said they were no better than they should be. They went traipsing off—alone, mind you!—to Chicago on buying trips and nobody knew what else.

Besides that, though Jessie Romaine had been born on a farm near Loyal, a little town a few miles north of Neillsville, she had lived in Milwaukee for a few years prior to her appearance in Neillsville. That was a period she chose not to talk about. Why, people wondered? (Just to give them something to talk about, I suspect.)

She wore hats with willow plumes on them; they were bigger and flashier than the other ladies considered circumspect. Her corsets were laced tighter, and if that wasn't rouge on her cheeks, then what was it? Jessie Romaine was putting on airs and calling attention to herself. Who did she think she was? Lillian Russell?

So before she even married Papa, the ladies of the town had already betrayed their disapproval by their reluctance to patronize her shop. She was on the verge of having to sell it—if anybody would buy it.

Papa bought it and shuttered it.

So Mamma tried to make a go of it as the wife of Sheriff Bob Eunson in his own bailiwick. His friends did not openly snub her, but they were cool, and Mamma was not one to take such coolness meekly. She never subscribed to the Beatitude that the meek shall inherit the earth.

My sister was a vexing problem too. Genevieve brooded over our own mother's replacement by a stepmother. She could never call anybody else Mamma. "Jessie" was disrespectful coming from a teen-ager, and they never hit upon an alternative quite satisfactory to either of them.

There was one way out of all this at the time: escape to the West. Genevieve would remain in Neillsville, at least until she finished high school next year. She was already in love with Larry Baker. She would probably marry him soon, and then she and Mamma could carry on a polite correspondence—Papa never wrote anybody. It would be easy to pretend they liked each other as long as the same roof did not cover them.

The more she thought about it, the better it all sounded to Mamma. The music of the words Frontier and Homestead, the Great Plains, the Great Divide, Buffalo Grass, even Blizzards made her tingle. What a Glorious Adventure! A Fresh Start. A New Scene. Wonderful New Friends, who had no cause to resent her. It would be a Veritable Fountain of Youth. Together the three of us would Conquer the Elements and Win the West! (Mamma thought and often spoke in such grandiloquent terms, especially when she was selling herself and Papa on some fallible project.) But whatever happened, it would be better, she must have thought when she lay awake alone at night, than the bitter taste of silent disapproval.

And so, he later told me, to please the handsome young

woman who had been good enough to marry him and become my mother, Papa broke with his past. He exchanged certain security during his declining years, good friends and loved relatives, the gentle landscape and greenery of the valley of the Black River, which he loved, for a homestead on dry land twenty miles northwest of Billings.

He went to Montana in the fall of 1910 and filed his claim. He made a deal with our new neighbor, Chris Gullard, to build us a shack. (Old Chris, as Papa called him, was also from Wisconsin—Osseo. He was a widower with two boys and two girls still living at home. "Salt of the earth," Papa said he was.) Then Papa came back to Neillsville, and we spent the next couple months getting ready for the move.

Early in December he loaded such worldly goods and livestock as were absolutely necessary onto a freight car and started West with it. Mamma managed to make Neillsville talk about her for the last time by insisting that we take the old black upright piano along. "Wouldn't Jessie Romaine just!" people said. "A piano on a dryland farm in Montana! Who's going to play it? Chief Sitting Bull?"

"Dale has a very nice touch," Mamma said smugly, having the last word. "I can teach him myself, until we find a professional teacher. I read music, you know."

We waited for Papa and the freight to get well ahead of us, and then Mamma and I went to St. Paul and boarded the Northern Pacific Limited for Billings.

I was already used to trains. I had ridden the cab of a locomotive from Neillsville to Marshfield one time, and the engineer, who was a friend of Papa's, had let me think I was pulling out the throttle. We glided into the round house

"A Piano on a Dryland Farm in Montana" 13

and sat there while the giant turntable majestically turned us all the way around so that we'd be headed in the right direction for the return trip.

But I had never slept in a berth on a train before. That was so exciting that I stayed awake all night. We set off well fortified with box lunches of fried chicken, sandwiches, hard-boiled eggs, and cake, but by the time we got to Mandan, North Dakota, we were patronizing the train butcher, who around about mealtime would board the train up front and, hawking his wares as he walked the aisle to the observation car, ride to the next stop.

Finally—as a special treat the last evening—we had supper in the diner. We had been due to arrive in Billings around ten o'clock that morning, which would have given us time to reach the homestead shortly after dark, but it was December, the engineer was coaxing his locomotive and ten groaning coaches into the teeth of a blizzard whistling down the Yellowstone, the water had frozen and cracked the N.P. water tower at Glendive, and a herd of cattle had drifted onto the tracks just outside Forsyth. We were by then nine hours late.

The lights in the diner were dim because, the brakeman explained, the bakehead, his derisive label for the fireman, was having trouble keeping up a head of steam on a day like this.

We could not see out the windows because they were white with forests and mountain ranges and canyons of frost. The clackety-clack of wheels on rails was hushed by the snow. We were eating dessert when the conductor came through, and Mamma asked him how long it would be before we got to Billings.

He took out his open-faced Hamilton watch and glanced

at it. "An hour and a half anyway you cut it," he said. "The slow speed we're making, you got plenty o' time to finish eating and get your duds on."

Then he paused, listening to a subtle change in the clatter of wheels on rails. "Yes sirree," he said. "that'll be the bridge over the Big Horn."

"The Big Horn," Mamma repeated, a note of awe in her voice. "Isn't that . . . wasn't that . . . ?"

The conductor nodded. "Mm-hmm. Just south of here a piece; where the Little Big Horn empties into it. All Crow Reservation nowadays. Not much to see." He turned and started off, calling "Custer . . . All out for Custer."

Mamma was staring at the frost on the window.

"Why didn't you and the conductor want me to know what you were talking about?" I asked.

"When you're older," Mamma said. "I don't think you'd be very interested now."

"Yeah," I said, "that's what you always say."

"Well, all right," she said, smiling and turning to me. "There was a massacre—Custer's Last Stand it's called."

"Who did he massacree?" I wanted to know.

"He didn't," she said. "The Indians massacred—not massacreed—him and his soldiers."

"Are any of the Indian braves still alive?"

"I suppose so. Some of them wouldn't be any older than Papa."

I blew on the window and finally made a hole in the frost. The conductor was right. There wasn't much to see—just snow streaking out of the dark.

Papa met us in Billings. It had stopped snowing, but the temperature was falling as it always did after a snow. "It's cold as Billy-be-damned," Papa said, hugging us both, "but I got us a good clean place to sleep and not in any high-toned hotel either."

The good clean place was the office of the livery stable owned by Al Reynolds. Papa had made arrangements to put up our team of horses, Sam and old Babe, and Molly, the cow. They had already been unloaded from the freight car. Al Reynolds was one damn fine fellow, Papa said. Him and Reynolds, why they got along like a couple of horse thieves. When Reynolds come to realize the train was going to be so damn late, he said why the bejesus didn't Papa bring his woman and his kid right over to the barn? We were welcome to bed down in the perfectly good bed his hostler slept in whenever him and his wife had a set-to and she tossed the little bastard out and locked the door on him. No sense catering to those stickup men at the Northern or the Commercial.

"Papa, honestly! Every other word?" Mamma said. "Hell, what did I say?" Papa asked.

Mamma sighed. She was too tired at the moment to resume her everlasting battle against his profanity, which was as natural and as innocent to him as breathing.

We all slept together with our clothes on, me on the outside, because the perfectly good bed sagged toward the middle and I would have been crushed otherwise. There were no sheets but plenty of blankets, and over them Papa tossed the shaggy buffalo robe he had brought from home. "Now it's back where it come from," he said. The robe must have weighed thirty pounds, but it did hold body heat. And that's all the heat there was in the room after the fire in the pot-bellied stove died out.

There was the clean, strong livery-stable odor of horses and harnesses and saddles and saddle oil and timothy and manure. Occasionally you could hear a horse pawing or rubbing against a stall. A Northern Pacific freight rumbled through, making the bed tremble. When it was out of hearing, a clock tolled ten. It was cold and unfriendly, not like our courthouse clock back home.

"I forgot to tell you, Mamma," Papa said. "Molly kicked the end of the piano. Left her hoof print on it."

"Did it do any damage?" I heard Mamma ask. "No, she seems to be fine," Papa said.

"I meant to the piano, Robert," Mamma said. She only called him by his full name when she was provoked.

"Oh, that," he said. "No, its innards seem to be all hunkydory."

A streetcar approached and stopped at the corner. A woman giggled and then laughed. A man's voice yelled, "Powder River, let 'er buck! Waaa-hooo!" Then footsteps crunched away unevenly in the snow.

"Some drunks," Papa said. "Ought to be locked up."

"Where's the bathroom?" I asked.

"Jeez," Papa said, "you ain't got to go?"

"No," I said. "I was just wondering—just in case."

"There ain't none in a barn," he said. "If you begin to feel like it, just think about something else."

"I'll try," I said. I shut my eyes and snuggled down beside him. His arm lay warm and protective across me. "I like Montana," I said sleepily.

"You ain't seen nothin' yet," Papa said. "Just wait till tomorrow. Why, it'll knock your eyes out."

"IT'S BUILT JUST LIKE MY SQUAW."

Two

My first sight of Billings by daylight was disappointing. Montana Avenue looked like the main streets I had seen back in Wisconsin. There were hitching posts and troughs for horses, stores, hotels, saloons and barber shops, jewelry stores and chop suey joints, and banks and more saloons. Billings might have been Eau Claire or Wausau, where Uncle Jim and Aunt Ella lived, except for a few Indians, the Stetson hats on some of the men, and the wall of rugged rim rocks that protected the town from the searing north winds.

Our homestead lay northwest of Billings. To reach it, you had to drive east until a break in the rim rocks permitted a turn to the north and access to the turbulent hills and sharp ravines that presently gave way to the high glacial plateau between the Yellowstone and the Musselshell rivers. The old stage road to the northwest tracked the original buffalo trail, which meandered from the plains down to the river. Not so long ago buffalo cows by the thousands had used it in spring to reach the early greening grass and drop their calves in relative protection from spring blizzards, coyotes, wolves, and bears.

We heated bricks over the stove in the livery stable, wrapped them in gunnysacks, and laid them in the bottom of the sled box. Mamma and I sat on a sack of potatoes to keep them from freezing and put our feet on the bricks, with the buffalo robe over our laps. Only our heads protruded above the top tier of the sled box, which was loaded with the necessities for the next week or so, until Papa could return to Billings for the rest of our goods.

Besides flour and cornmeal, ham and bacon and canned goods, there was a cookstove, a bed, a cot (for me), a few chairs, a kitchen table, a couple of lamps and a lantern, a shotgun, a Singer sewing machine and Mamma's buxom dress form propped up at the very back. This last made an indelible impression on a fat Indian riding a moth-eaten mustang. He approached warily and stopped to stare at the stiff, headless apparition.

"My name's Eunson. Bob Eunson," Papa said.

"Name Joe," the Indian muttered, still not taking his eyes off the dress form. Most Indians were named Joe, I discovered. Or perhaps they only said they were to keep conversation to the minimum they preferred.

"Meet my wife and boy," Papa said.

The Indian raised his hand in salute without looking at

"It's Built Just Like My Squaw"

us. Then he pointed at the dress form. Papa's eyes followed Joe's gaze. "Oh, that," Papa said, scratching his head. He turned to Mamma. "Stand up, Jessie," he said.

Mamma would ordinarily have wanted to know what for, but she was uneasy around Indians, even fat, old ones like Joe. The grim stories of scalpings were not yet safely embalmed by history. Mamma stood up.

"See?" Papa said, pointing from Mamma to the dress form. "It's built just like my squaw. She makes her clothes on it."

This made little sense to the Indian, who continued to watch warily until our trail dropped into a gully and he lost sight of us. Then Mamma gave Papa what for, for referring to her as his squaw.

In a crate under the kitchen table were a dozen chickens, eleven Plymouth Rock hens, and a rooster. Eggs would freeze and crack before you could get them home—Robinson's little store and post office at Acton was five miles from the homestead—and though hens laid only sporadically in winter, at least we would have an occasional fresh egg for breakfast.

As for milk, Molly, our black-and-white Holstein, stumbled along behind us, cowlike and docile, her small cloven hooves breaking through a snow crust that would support the weight of a horse.

When we first set out, Shep had been startled by the motion of the sled and jumped overboard into the snow. I had wanted to stop and go back for him, but Papa said if he were our dog he'd follow us. If he weren't, we might as well find out about it right off.

I kept calling him, but he sat there in the road staring at us until we were almost out of sight. Then he made up his mind we were his family and raced after us, one ear flapping. He passed the sled, capered and barked at Sam and old Babe—"Damn fool pup!" Papa laughed—then made a few mischievous dashes back to nip at Molly's heels, and finally came alongside and begged to be taken into the sled again. He stayed there, asleep on my feet, for mile after endless mile unmarked by any sign of habitation.

The sun hung white and cold just above the southern horizon, which at first was jagged and speckled with a few leafless cottonwoods. The road presently began to climb and then narrowed to hug the perpendicular north wall of a little canyon. There was no room for rigs to pass each other and you could not see more than fifty feet ahead because of the convexity of the canyon wall. Papa yelled a warning to any unseen traveler who might be approaching from the northwest: "Hold your horses! We're comin' round!"

There was no answer except an echo from the south wall, so we started ahead. There was nothing frightening about it until Papa told us this was called Holdup Hill. Before the Great Northern built its branch line from Billings to Great Falls two years ago this whole area had been serviced by stagecoaches. Because of its peculiar formation and the fact that there was no other passage to the north except around this canyon wall, it had become a favorite spot for holdups. Even one loner could do the job because a stagecoach, suddenly confronted by a gunman from around the bend ahead, had no choice but to stop and hand over whatever valuables it might be transporting.

Somehow that account scared the daylights out of me. Afterward, whenever we approached Holdup Hill, I would shut my eyes and refuse to open them until Papa said we were well past it.

After Holdup Hill the landscape began to flatten out. It was still wrinkled and mussed, however, as if a gigantic flatiron, heated for wool, had been carelessly run across a white cotton sheet that had not even been sprinkled first. The sheet was soiled with sagebrush and greasewood signs, Papa said, of alkali and gumbo soil, where nothing much but prairie dogs and rattlesnakes would grow.

There was no sagebrush, no greasewood, up on the rim, he said with pride. Nothing but grass in rich, loose soil a foot thick, beautiful buffalo grass, which was so heavy even the snows of winter could not flatten it out. Spring rains turned it green, and spring breezes rippled it like the waves of the sea, Al Reynolds had told him.

Along about noon we passed a cowhand who volunteered that he had had a bellyful of Montana. He was going back east to Nebraska and marry the richest widow woman who would take him on.

And in midafternoon we met the Moodys. Mrs. Moody's face was set in a grimace of pain. She had a tooth that had been acting up and stubbornly resisting the benison of hot salt bags and oil of cloves. "So," Mr. Moody said, "I just says to myself, we'll drive to Billings and have 'em yank it out and put the old lady out of her misery."

The "old lady" was probably under forty. If she had many more teeth out, she said, she would need a set of uppers. She hated the thought.

"Nothing to it," Papa said. "Had mine out when I was younger'n you even. Not a toothache since, and that's the God's truth!"

"Where you folks going to live?" Mrs. Moody asked,

cupping a hand over her mouth so the cold air would not aggravate the ache.

"Up on the rim," Papa said. "Just north of them Norwegians. Damn! What's their names?"

"Gullard?" Mr. Moody suggested. "Chris Gullard?"

"That's it," Papa said. "Gillard."

"No, Gullard," Mr. Moody corrected him.

"Yeah, like I say—Gillard," Papa said. Once he got a name wrong, wild horses could not change him. The Gullards remained the Gillards for as long as we lived in Montana.

"Scandihoovians. Nice folks," Mr. Moody said. "We're neighbors, too," Mrs. Moody said.

Mamma said that would be nice. She didn't know there would be anybody close by right at first. "How far is your place from ours?"

"Five miles, I'd say," Mr. Moody said. "Just a whoop and a holler out here. Anything we can do, anything you want to borry till you get settled, you just name it."

We drove on. After a while we caught sight of the glistening steel of the Great Northern branch, which seemed to spring out of the shimmering white earth and then unroll into an infinity of frosting, an infinity that presently sprouted an unpainted, empty house off to the right and, far beyond it to the left, a railroad station.

That, Papa said, was our address: Acton. Nothing much there except a little depot for protection against the elements while you waited to flag down the train; a water tower, and a shack for section hands. Nobody lived there. The post office was the concession of a man named Robinson, a dryland farmer who had built his buildings a mile to the west because that's where the diviner told him he would strike water, hopefully without alkali in it. Once a day Charley Robinson collected the mail sack tossed off the train at Acton, and once a day the passing mail car hooked onto the heavy canvas sack, which he suspended from its stanchion alongside the track.

Robinson and his missus were real hustlers, Papa said. Last fall they had told him they were going to turn their front room into a little grocery store. They never had time to sit down anyhow, so they might as well get some good out of their sitting room, they said. It would be convenient for folks while they squatted on their claims. They wouldn't have to go all the way to Comanche or Broadview just for chicken feed or cheese and beans and gopher traps and such.

We veered off to the right a few hundred yards before we reached Acton. The sun was growing fat on the southwest horizon. Already distant mountain peaks were sawing into its soft pink underbelly. I asked Papa what the mountains were and he said they were the Absorkies, and so they were to Papa all the time we lived there. Other people might call them the Absarokas, but that didn't cut any ice with him.

The bricks beneath our feet had cooled off long before we commenced the slow, steady climb to the top of the rim, where our homestead lay. The rim itself was a glacial formation two or three hundred feet above the surrounding flats. To the south it dropped off in sharp cliffs, but to the north and east it dribbled into ravines and gullies, which, Papa said, grew the only timber closer than the Yellowstone Valley—not forests such as we had known in Wisconsin, but plenty of firewood, pine big enough for log cabins, and cedar for fence posts. To the west and southwest the glacier had ground the original cliff down to a gentle slope.

As we rose higher and higher, the sagebrush thinned out. A jackrabbit, white as the snow, appeared out of nowhere and bounced playfully ahead of the team. He seemed to want company, or perhaps merely protection from the gray wolf that Papa pointed out lying near a reddish-beige smudge in the snow. That smudge had been a live antelope when we left Billings this morning. The wolf's eyes tracked us, but he was too satiated to move. Papa considered taking a shot at the predator, but his shotgun would not reach that far and the explosion would probably scare the horses more than the wolf.

Near the crest of the hill Papa yelled "Whoa!" He turned around and peered off to the southwest. Mamma and I turned to look too. As far as you could see there was nothing. Not even a cloud. Nothing but a flat, endless white plain, split from southeast to northwest by a railroad track as straight as a light ray. All that was left of the sun was a purple haze on the horizon, the evening star already blinking through the indigo to the east.

"That's Montana for you," Papa said. "Before too long there'll be farmhouses and big red barns all acrost there." His right arm swept from south to north as his imagination turned this bleak landscape into Wisconsin. "And silos. And granaries. And corncribs. Trees. Fences, too. People," he said. "More people, that's what this damn wilderness needs."

"Well, here are three more," Mamma said, putting an arm around my shoulders.

"That's a fact," Papa said, missing the subtle import of her statement, "but we won't stay around here long enough to see it. We'll be proved up and back to God's country long afore they tame all this."

"We'll see," Mamma said. Like so many of Mamma's pronouncements, this one was open to at least two interpretations. If she was called on one, she could slide behind another. "We'll see" could mean that within fourteen months the whole landscape would undergo a transformation, or We'll see whether we ever go back to Wisconsin at all. I suspected it meant the latter and that Mamma was tactfully postponing what nowadays would be called a confrontation.

"Still and all," Papa said, taking one last look before turning back to the horses, "it kind of takes your breath away."

"That's the altitude," Mamma said. "We're not used to it."

From the distance somewhere ahead came the bark of a dog, a strange bark that turned into a wail almost like a woman crying. Mamma's arm tightened around my shoulder, and suddenly Shep was standing up, the fur on his back bristling. "Coyote," Papa said, and clucked to the horses.

But Sam and old Babe had no more than eased the slack out of the tugs when Shep leaped out of the sled. "The wolf will get him and eat him!" I yelled. "Here Shep, here Shep!"

"He doesn't know his name yet," Mamma reminded me.

"He don't know who flung dung," Papa said disgustedly. He jumped off the sled, slipped and fell. It made him mad. "Come here, you damn fool!" he called. And presently Shep did, and Papa, who had sounded as if he would tear the pup apart, picked him up and petted him and brought him back to the sled. "Now hang onto him!" he grumbled, tossing Shep into my lap.

He climbed into the sled and clucked to the horses, not noticing that in the interval Molly, weary from trudging eighteen miles during the last six hours, had lain down. It took another five minutes to get her on her feet, and Papa was fit to be tied. When he finally hoisted himself back into the sled, I started to ask him how much farther it would be to the homestead, but Mamma whispered that I'd better not pester him with any question yet awhile.

"IT WILL BE FINE AND DANDY WHEN WE GET IT FIXED UP."

Three

The fertile plateau of the rim was roughly three miles across and four from its jagged eastern declivities to the gentle sweep into the gumbo flats to the west. Though there were ravines and gullies in section 29 to the north of us, most of the land rolled gently like vast ground swells in a petrified sea.

To the east and north our immediate view from the shack was cut off by one of these ground swells, but look to the west and there was Comanche, seven miles off, but in that crystal-clear atmosphere, right on our doorstep. Comanche claimed a population of some fifty souls, huddled together for their own private reasons and trying to eke out a living along the railroad track in the sticky and sterile gumbo.

Turn your gaze a little farther to the north and west, and there stood Broadview, a metropolis relatively twice as large as Comanche. Broadview, up out of the alkali and gumbo, was booming. It already boasted a grain elevator and was a scheduled stop on the Great Northern branch The land around it was under cultivation and the dryland farmers had been lulled by merciful weather and bumper crops the last couple years. Many had gone into debt to buy up the six-hundred-and-forty-acre sections, which the government in an excess of generosity had lavished on the railroads to encourage them to open up the West. Shacks, even a few more or less permanent farmhouses and outbuildings, already dotted the prairie around Broadview.

Beyond Comanche, beyond Broadview, must surely be the end of the world, the jumping-off place, but we could not see it because the land rolled on forever, punctuated here and there by a black butte, its jagged buttresses intricately carved by tireless chisels of wind and rain and ice and snow, or a small white cloud gathering courage to sail across the dome of the sky, or a herd of grazing white-faced longhorns or sometimes a sheepherder's wagon in the center of the swirling galaxy of his sheep.

(Sheepherders were a breed apart. If they had not been peculiar characters to begin with, they soon turned loco, everyone said, from listening to nothing but the wind and the day-and-night bleating of sheep. They were mostly dirty, long-haired, unshaven, and rancid. "That's what happens to little boys who forget to wash behind their ears," Mamma used to say.)

Our shack was 12 by 20, its outer walls and curved

steamboat roof covered with black tarpaper which would hopefully insulate its rough pine siding and roofing from the weather. When the three of us—and Shep—walked into it that first evening, it was empty except for a pot-bellied stove and a stack of firewood, which the Gullards had provided. Everything else we could bring with us, Papa had told them last fall, but chances were we'd need some heat first thing.

Mamma let out a little gasp and leaned against the wall for a minute.

Papa was slicing kindling with his jackknife. "Guess I didn't warn you sufficient," he said.

She swallowed hard a couple times and then managed a dismal smile. "It's all *right,*" she said, convincing herself. "It will be fine and dandy when we get it fixed up—lace curtains *there,* our Maxfield Parrish *there* . . ." She glanced around, her eyes a little frantic, as if to find some other topic while she got her breathing under control. Her gaze lit on Shep. "What is that dog *doing!*" she cried.

What Shep was doing was lifting his leg and putting his calling card on Papa's overshoe.

"Git!" Papa said, swatting at him with his mitten.

Shep hid behind me and peered out at Papa. Only his blue watch-eye was visible in the light of the lantern. "He won't do it again," I said. "Will you, Shep?"

Shep wagged his tail and looked properly ashamed of himself. He seemed to be begging foregiveness. We soon learned that was one of his best tricks. The sight was too much for Mamma and Papa. They both started to laugh. When they finally stopped, Papa said, "I'm sorry, Jessie. You didn't know it was going to be like this, did you?"

"Who cares?" she said, and you could tell from the way

she said it that now she didn't. It was just that the first shock of the empty little box of a cabin with its naked two-by-fours had thrown her. "Let's get a move on," she said, slapping her hands together. "There's a lot to be done before we can lie down."

"We'll just bring in what we've got to have for tonight. Some bread and butter. Tomorrow I'll ride over to the Gillards and get one of the boys to lend a hand with the cookstove," Papa said.

"I'm strong, I can lift," Mamma said. "We don't want to be beholden."

"Hell, they're neighbors," Papa said. "They'd think we was standoffish if we didn't ask them to lend us a hand when we need it."

"When we need it, yes," Mamma agreed, "but let's not get in the habit of . . ."

There was a knock on the door. Papa opened it, and there stood Chris Gullard. Mr. Gullard—or old Chris, as Papa always referred to him—had been born in Norway. He was about sixty, a small man of Papa's height, with flowing white mustaches. Asthma had plagued him all his life.

Behind him stood his lanky sons, Harry and Carl. Harry was twenty, and Carl seventeen. All three wore sheepskin coats, caps with fur-lined earlappers, and overalls with the legs buckled into overshoes.

"Ve yust come by to see is some'ting ve can do." Mr. Gullard spoke in the soft musical cadence of the Norwegians.

"We're much obliged," Mamma said, "but . . ."

"Damn right we're much obliged!" Papa said, shaking

hands all round. "And there surer'n hell is something you can do. But how'd you folks know we got here?"

Harry, it seemed, had sauntered up the rocky knoll back of their house to get a better look at the spectacular display of northern lights and had noticed a sled with a cow tied to it passing half a mile away. "I calculated that had to be you folks," Harry said.

"So," Mr. Gullard said, "ve come. Show us where to stow things."

"I WOULDN'T GIVE OLEOMARGARINE TO A DOG!"

Four

It was an open winter, with Montana turning a deceptively mild and gentle face on the tenderfeet from Wisconsin. See, it seemed to be saying, don't believe everything you hear about blizzards and killer north winds. That's a lot of bunk. And look at those plains, will you! No trees to fell, no stumps to pull up or burn before you can even get to the land to cultivate it. Why, there lies that rich soil beneath a foot of snow, just waiting for a benign Chinook wind to reveal it to the plowshare!

On his third trip to Billings Papa brought back the walking plow. We were not planning to sow any grain come spring—what was the point when we were to be here for only one growing season?—but we would need a vegetable garden, and we could probably peddle off a secondhand plow to some other homesteader after we proved up.

Pure, clean mineral water bubbled up from Buffalo Spring on Al Reynolds's homestead about a mile northwest of us. It was the only water on the rim—unless you wanted to dig for it—but we were welcome. All we had to do was hitch old Babe to the stoneboat, roll an empty barrel onto it, go for the water, and fetch it home.

There was fresh meat for the shooting—rabbits, venison, pheasant, prairie chicken, and sage hen, though you had to be hungrier than we ever were to eat that last. We tried once, but it was tough and stringy and gamey. Shep had to finish it off. (Shep would eat anything you gave him and a lot of things you didn't, though he preferred leftover buckwheat pancakes. I could toss them at him from ten feet, and he'd catch and inhale one after another as long as they kept coming.)

Within a few days almost all our new neighbors had come by. Most of them were from Wisconsin like us. Besides the Gullards (the two girls, Manda and Selma, were coming out from Osseo as soon as school let out next spring), there was Earl Hickson, a good-looking young Irishman who had been a cowboy for Al Reynolds and earning forty dollars a month. He had decided that even good wages like that left something to be desired, so he filed a claim on a hundred and sixty acres a couple miles southeast of us, just beyond the choice section 33, which was one of many that belonged to the Northern Pacific.

Earl was lonesome and tired of batching it all winter. Nobody had to ask him twice to stay to Sunday dinner, which, of course, was the noon meal—supper was at six. Papa told Earl that I had a seventeen-year-old sister who might come out for a visit next summer, and Earl allowed as how he'd be willing to try to think up ways to help her pass the time.

Northeast of us Ed Ives, his son, Dan, and his son-in-law, Wert Barney, had filed on adjoining homesteads. They had all pitched in together and raised log cabins within hollering distance of each other. While Papa hit it off with the Iveses and Wert Barney, Mamma did not fare so well with their womenfolk. She read disapproval in the way they stared at the piano, which Papa had hauled out from storage by the time they came to call. When I showed off by playing "The March of the Wee Folk," Mrs. Ives, Senior, raised her eyebrows and declared that she had never heard of a little boy playing the piano before.

Mamma gave her a bright smile and said, "Well, Mrs. Ives, now you can tell folks you've heard of one, can't you?"

"They just came to snoop," Mamma said after the Iveses had gone.

"Now, Jessie," Papa said.

"And do you know what they brought as a housewarmer? Oleomargarine! A keg of white oleomargarine. Why, it looks just like lard! If they think I'll put *that* on johnnycake!"

Papa explained that Mr. Ed Ives had noticed that old Molly had dried up; she wouldn't freshen until May.

"Well, just because we live in a tarpaper shack do they think we can't afford to *buy* butter?"

"They didn't mean any harm," I said.

"Why, I wouldn't give oleomargarine to a dog!"

"I bet Shep would eat it, though," I said.

(I tried him later. He would.)

And then there was Peterson. He had a given name,

John, but I never heard him called anything but Peterson. He was a big, gregarious Norwegian from Minnesota, about forty years old and without visible ties to anyone. He lived in a dugout. He said he'd dug himself the hole in the ground, lowered a stove and a bed in it, and pulled in the hole after him. When you approached his place north of Buffalo Spring the only thing you could see till you were almost on top of it was a black stovepipe sticking up out of the ground.

"He tipples," Mamma whispered to me after he had paid us his first call.

"How can you tell?"

"Why, he smells like a brewery," she said, but there was no note of condemnation in her voice. Mamma was one of those women who will overlook almost anything in a man, but let one of her own sex step over the mark and watch out! "Poor man," she told Papa. "Some woman is obviously to blame."

"How'd you figure that?"

"Well, why else would a nice-looking man like that be living underground like a prairie dog?"

Mamma was a master—or perhaps a slave—of the not quite nonsequitur. Present her with a situation and she would draw a conclusion that satisfied her perfectly, while it completely befuddled her listeners. Such a conclusion subsequently became solid fact that would, in turn, support almost any further assumption.

The claim adjoining ours on the west belonged to a spinster, Julia Adams, who was acquiring title the easy way. Instead of a straight fourteen-month residence, she lived on the land for six months out of each year over a three-year period.

Then, scattered about, were various members of the Blodgett clan and the Torpens, who had several children, the only ones on the rim except for me. And later, Selma Gullard.

And finally there was the rather dashing and alliteratively named Niles Newcomb, whose land we had to cross to reach Buffalo Spring. And old Mr. Kimball.

Mr. Kimball did not ride over to say Howdy. The Gullards said he wouldn't; he never called on anybody and made it pretty clear that he didn't want anybody to call on him. Nobody knew why. He lived in a tarpaper shack like ours. Sometimes when we passed by we'd see smoke rising from the stovepipe. Other times there was no sign of life.

Papa said it wasn't natural for a man to keep to himself that way—even a sheepherder had sheep around to swear at when he felt down in the mouth. The poor soul could kick the bucket and nobody would know it for months.

So Papa, who loved everybody under a sort of blanket of goodwill toward all mankind, stopped by one day. He knocked on the door and waited, but Mr. Kimball—who must have been inside and alive because smoke was coming out of the stovepipe—never showed himself. Finally Papa yelled, "My name's Bob Eunson. We're neighbors. If you ever need help, you let us know, do you hear?"

Mr. Kimball must have heard, but he kept his silence. Charley Robinson, the postmaster-storekeeper west of Acton, was the only man who knew him at all. He said Mr. Kimball would walk in once a month to pick up his mail, mostly a letter or two from his niece, some actress named Clara Kimball Young. There was sometimes a check for twenty-five dollars in one of the letters, and Mr. Robinson would cash it.

"THERE GOES

VESUVIUS!"

Five

"You know something?" Papa said one day. "I don't think that dog's any too damn bright." Shep had discovered rabbit tracks and instead of following them was frantically digging a hole in the snow as if the rabbit were buried there.

"He's just a pup," I said. "You got to remember that."

"Let's see if we can teach him to retrieve," Papa said. He was through forking the manure out of the barn stalls, and I had gathered the eggs—two to be exact—after finishing my daily lessons with Mamma. She had brought my second-grade textbooks from Wisconsin, along with such literary staples as *The Wizard of Oz, Freckles, The Girl of the*

Limberlost, Little Women, The Shepherd of the Hills, and of course *Black Beauty* and *The Dog of Flanders.* I was not to grow up without culture.

Shep did not look or act at all like Patrasche, the dog of Flanders. While his left ear now stood erect like the right and his puppy coat had been replaced by sleek black fur, he did not seem to realize that he was a work dog. Life was merely a romp.

Papa picked up a stick, spat on it, let Shep sniff it, and then threw it. "Go get it, Shep," he cried.

Shep wagged his tail amiably and sat down. Papa shook his head. "I'll show him," I said. "Come on, Shep."

He trotted alongside me, and I showed him the stick in the snow. "Pick it up," I said, looking back over my shoulder and hoping Papa would not see how obtuse Shep was being. Then I picked up the stick and put it in his mouth. "He's got the idea now," I said.

I had a little trouble getting the stick out of his mouth again, but he finally opened his jaws. Now I spat on it, let him sniff it, and then heaved it as hard as I could. It sailed all the way over the barn. "Go git it," I said. "Go git it, Shep!"

This time he seemed to have got it through his head. He disappeared around the barn. "Gee," I said, "he's sure one fast learner."

We waited for him to come back with the stick. And waited. Presently there was the sound of hysterics from the chicken coop, which was merely partitioned off from the barn. ("If we stay here," Mamma had once said, "we'll have to build a separate hen house. It's not heathy to subject livestock to chicken lice." "But we're not going to stay, so that's none of our never mind," Papa had answered.)

"What the hell?" Papa said. "Did that damn dog get in the chicken coop?"

"No," I said nervously, "he couldn't even if he was a mind to. That's the rooster chasing one of the hens. You know how he does."

I had no more than said it when Shep raced around the corner of the barn. He had something white in his mouth. He trotted happily up to us as if to say: See? I got the idea. What he finally relinquished was the glass nest egg left in the nest to encourage the hens to lay their eggs there instead of on the ground.

"I must have forgot to latch the chicken coop door," I said.

I took the nest egg back and put it where Shep had found it. When I came out of the barn, Papa was looking down at Shep and shaking his head. "Lucky it wasn't a real egg," he said.

"Why?"

"He'd a busted it and might've got a taste for raw eggs."

"Oh, he won't never get a real egg," I said. "I'll watch him careful." We started off toward the shack with Shep frolicking along in front of us. "But what would we do if he did?"

"You can't keep a dog like that," Papa said. "You got to get rid of a suck-egg dog."

"You wouldn't!" I said

"We'll cross that bridge when there's water under it." He sighed and then, just before we opened the door, he lowered his voice. "No need to let on to Mamma what happened. It'd just worry her."

There was something new in the air.

Though still early in March, the wind out of the west

turned gentle and soft and balmy, and patches of earth pushed through the snow.

The arrival of the Chinook at just this time was a good omen, Mamma said conspiratorially, because Aunt Edie and Uncle Corve were coming to visit us for a few days during Uncle Corve's vacation. It would be nice for them to see Montana at its best.

Mamma obviously had something up her sleeve. Aunt Edie was her eldest sister—there had been four Romaine girls—and when she married Corve Ransimer, they went West and settled in Coeur d'Alene in the nineties. While I had never seen either of them, I was in awe of Uncle Corve because of the eminence of his profession. He was a motorman, and not your run-of-the-mill motorman at that. He piloted a streetcar back and forth between Spokane, Washington, and Coeur d'Alene, Idaho, which gave him, in my eyes, only slightly less status than that of a locomotive engineer, which, of course, was far more impressive than being President of the United States.

Uncle Corve proved out to be not quite what I expected. He was big and fat and jolly, a hearty eater, and after meals a formidable belcher. When he erupted, Aunt Edie would cluck reprovingly and say, "There goes Vesuvius!" "Excuse me," Uncle Corve would say, frowning and pounding his stomach as if it were a pesky reflex completely beyond his control.

What disappointed me at first about Uncle Corve was that he did not consider his profession an enviable one. "It don't go nowhere," he said.

"But gosh, you go to Spokane every day."

"Yup," he said. "Twicet-a-day . . . and back. It gets monotonous. And your Aunt Edie and me—well, we're not gettin' any younger."

Mamma had precisely the solution for that, she said. Why didn't they come to Montana and file a claim? "We'd be . . . *near*—like real sisters again. It's not as if you had children in school to keep you tied down there."

Aunt Edie and Uncle Corve exchanged glances. Then we all went outside, Papa and Uncle Corve in their shirtsleeves, because it was so unseasonably warm. (Uncle Corve's shirt was striped with shiny red silk, the sleeves held up by red, white, and blue sleeveholders.) Mamma took snapshots of us with her 2A Brownie to send to the relatives in Wisconsin to prove what it was like in Acton, Montana, in March 1911.

That night I heard Aunt Edie and Uncle Corve whispering. (Papa and Mamma gave them the bed, Mamma slept on my cot, and Papa and I on the floor.)

Next morning the Chinook was still with us, the snow almost gone, and the sky noisy with wedges of wild geese honking their way north. Papa and Uncle Corve saddled up the horses and took off as soon as the chores and breakfast were out of the way. When they returned around five that afternoon, Uncle Corve said he'd found just the spot he'd been looking for all his born days. It was only ten miles away—on the slope the other side of Acton.

Mamma and Aunt Edie hugged each other and laughed and cried. This was going to change everything, Mamma confided to her sister. With family here, Robert wouldn't be so all-fired anxious to go back to Neillsville at the end of the fourteen months, three of which were already ticked off on the calendar.

"Corve and I wouldn't want to make such a big move," Aunt Edie said when she and Mamma were alone together fixing supper, "if you folks were going back East next winter."

"We're not," Mamma said.

"You sure?"

Mamma took a deep breath and nodded. "Don't let on I told you."

"But Bob sounds as if he's hankering for Wisconsin."

Mamma looked around and saw me poring over one of the funny papers Uncle Corve had brought from Spokane.

"Dale, what are you doing there behind the stove?"

"Reading," I said. "About Buster Brown and Tige." Tige was Buster Brown's bulldog. When Buster got in trouble, he could always blame it on Tige.

"The chicken coop needs whitewashing."

"No, it doesn't. I already whitewashed it this morning."

"Then run outside and play."

"There's nobody to play with."

Mamma turned to Aunt Edie. "That's one of the disadvantages," she said. "No children anywhere near his age. Of course Chris Gullard has an eleven-year-old daughter coming out this spring."

"She's a girl," I said.

"But all that will change in a year or so," Mamma said to Aunt Edie.

"You mean Selma Gullard is going to turn into a boy?"

"I mean nothing of the sort and you know it! Now go throw rocks for Shep."

I would hear no more about what Mamma was finagling, so I went outside. Shep was waiting on the stoop, as he always was. You take your average farm dog and he'd have been off in the field with the menfolks, especially when one of them had a gun, but not old Shep. Papa was showing Uncle Corve where he thought he'd dig a well if there was time this spring and he had taken the shotgun along in case they flushed a prairie hen.

I threw rocks for a while, being careful to throw them in the opposite direction from the chicken coop—Shep might go inside and retrieve another egg. Then we had another lesson in handshaking, but he was not very good at it yet. I'd shake his hand, then he'd put my hand in his mouth and shake it.

Once a dog gets off on the wrong foot about something, Papa said, skip it for a while and do something else. I went back into the shack very quietly just in time to hear Mamma say, "I'd shoot myself rather than go back."

"Oh, prunes and piffle! That's just *you* talking, Jessie," Aunt Edie said.

"You don't *know* me." Then Mamma heard me. "I thought you went out to play," she said, cross.

I told her I was tired of playing and would rather practice my reading. She looked around the room, grabbed a book, and thrust it into my hands. "All right," she said. "Go read it. But read it outside and don't come back until I tell you to."

Sulking at the reprimand, I went outside. Shep followed me to the top of the rise in front of the shack. It was almost sunset and half of Montana unrolled before us. The gumbo flats this side of Comanche had turned into a dirty lake since the thaw, but now it was pure gold. A freight train no bigger than a worm crawled along toward Broadview.

Shep pricked up his ears at the sound of Papa's shotgun. I told him it was nothing to be scared of, then sat down on a rock and opened the book Mamma had given me to page 90. I had not yet reached the point where reading in silence made any sense. It was not really happening unless I spoke the words aloud.

"Even with eyes protected by the green spectacles," I read slowly, "Dorothy and her friends were at first dazzled by the brilliancy of the wonderful City."

Shep lay at my feet, his eyes intent and questioning on my face. It was not fair to him, I realized, to start reading a story right in the middle, so I told him about the land of Oz and how a cyclone carried Dorothy there and why even dogs had to wear glasses before they dared to look at the Emerald City. "Because, you see," I said, and commenced reading slowly again, " 'the streets were lined with beautiful houses all built of green marble and studded everywhere with sparkling emeralds.' "

Shep cocked his head as if to ask, "Why didn't they wear specks?" and I said they did, I had read that, and he had not been listening.

Neither of us was aware that Papa and Uncle Corve had come back—without a prairie chicken; Papa was not a very good shot—and were standing watching us. Apparently Uncle Corve was a little worried. Having no children of his own, the sight of a child reading aloud to a dog was unsettling.

"It's just that the boy's got nobody to play with," Papa said.

"I hope you're right," Uncle Corve said, not fully convinced.

We walked on down to the barn. Uncle Corve sat on a sawhorse, basking in the warm twilight while Papa went inside and scattered fresh straw, which came from the Gullard's strawstack, on the ground. I watched him. He didn't have much to say except to warn me away from the horses' heels. "Never come up on a horse from the back without speaking to him first," he said for the hundredth time.

"I know, Papa," I said.

By the time he was through bedding down the animals, Uncle Corve had walked on up to the shack. Papa seemed in no hurry; he had something on his mind.

"You like it out here, Dale?" he finally asked.

"I like it fine," I said.

"You don't want to go back to Neillsville?"

"Gosh, I don't know."

"I should think you'd miss Lewis Williamson and Theodore Brameld and your other friends."

"Yeah, I guess," I said. "But I got Shep."

He bent over and put his hand on Shep's head. "Yeah," he said, "you got Shep." Then he didn't say anything for quite a while. "Your mamma wants to settle out here permanent," he finally said.

"Oh," I said, as if I didn't know.

"She's got it in for Neillsville," he said. "Someday you'll understand."

Both of us stood looking off past Broadview, which by now had swallowed up the freight train. Beyond it, and beyond that butte over there, it occurred to me, must be the Land of Oz, because there was suddenly a bright green flash in the western sky. The book said the sky above the City was tinted green and the rays of the sun were green too.

"Papa, did you know they got green popcorn in the Land of Oz?" I asked him.

Papa did not seem to hear. "Your mamma's a mighty good woman," he said after a little while. "She's making you a first-rate mother, and I want to do anything within reason to keep her contented."

"Gee," I said, "I don't even remember when we didn't have Mamma."

Papa looked down at me and smiled. "That's probably all for the best," he said. "But sometimes—oh, just sometimes—I can't help wishin' you could remember your own mother."

"Genevieve remembers," I said.

"Yes," he sighed. "Genevieve remembers."

Then we started up toward the house. "If we decide to stay up here on the rim," he ruminated, "there's one hell of a lot to be done."

"PRAISE GOD
FROM WHOM
ALL BLESSINGS FLOW."

Six

Spring came in on the heels of the Chinook.
Meadowlarks warbled and nested in the greening buffalo grass, and the drab slope east of the shack turned into a pink blanket of bitterroot. The air itself was perfumed with wild roses and even the ugly cactus celebrated the rite by hiding its sharp spines under blatant red and yellow and purple bouquets.
When the soil was just right, not too wet and not too dry, Papa hitched old Babe and Sam to the plow. Mamma held the reins while Papa gripped the plow handles and tilted the plowshare into the sod. Plowing was a task he had never done before, and he had to learn by trial and

error. He took a deep breath and said, "Well, here goes nothin', Jessie."

She clucked to the team and slapped them on the rumps with the ends of the reins. The horses leaned their big shoulders into their collars and the plowshare lunged into the virgin earth, rending and tearing the age-old roots. Behind us—I walked along in the furrow with Shep—rolled a fourteen-inch ribbon, which turned from black to chocolate to cinnamon as the rays of the warm sun sucked up the winter moisture. No doubt about it; this was good, rich soil.

At first the plow jumped and bucked in Papa's hands and threatened to break his arms, but before long he got the hang of it, the ribbon straightened out, and the furrow maintained a constant depth of four inches. Once in a while Mamma would let out a yip when she stepped on a cactus and one of the needles penetrated soft Eastern shoes that were never meant for such rough work. Then we would stop while she took off her shoes and yanked the needles out of them. By the time there were three rows of upturned sod, Mamma could use that to walk on. Her feet sank into it, but that was better than risking the cactus when she kept to the left of the plow.

By midafternoon I was tired, so they let me ride the arched back of the plow. Papa, whose hands were blistering under his gloves, said there was no danger now. There was nothing to plowing, he said. Just use a little horse sense instead of bull strength and awkwardness.

We were heading back on the last furrow of the day when Mamma yelled "Snakes!" dropped the reins, and took off across the field, hell-bent for election. Papa grabbed me off the plow and tossed me ten feet, but it didn't hurt because I landed on the new-turned sod. What had happened was that the plowshare had sliced through a nest of still-hibernating snakes, and there they were, their parts lashing out everywhichway.

They were harmless bullsnakes, but that didn't cut much ice with Mamma. To her a snake was a *snake,* whether it rattled or hissed or swam, and she did not even turn around to look back until she was forty or fifty feet away. What she saw, what we all saw and could do nothing about was Shep grabbing one and then another in his mouth and shaking the daylights out of them. "Cut that out!" Papa said, and made a swipe at him.

"Come here, Shep!" Mamma yelled, which was her big mistake, because for once he obeyed—with a foot-long wienie of wriggling bullsnake in his mouth. He tried to catch up to her, but she beat him to the shack and slammed the door before he could lay his prize at her feet.

That was the last time Mamma ever walked along beside the plow and drove the team, but it did not much matter, because Papa had it down pat. He could wrap the reins around his shoulders and guide the team by yelling "Gee" and "Haw," and hold the plow steady in the ground at the same time.

He plowed about forty acres, never once mentioning that we had not intended to put in a crop this year at all. Then he went to Billings and brought home a disc and iron-tooth drag, and when the harrowing was done, the three of us sowed the field by hand, scattering the seed onto the spring breeze. (Papa said he did not aim to spend money on a seeder yet, just in case something happened and we did not stay.) Then he dragged the field once more to cover the seed—twenty-five acres of wheat, ten of oats, and five of alfalfa—and we prayed for rain.

It rained—a gentle rain right from heaven. God called it off when we'd had enough and turned on the sun.

I did not carry enough body weight to help Papa dig the well, so he hired Carl Gullard at a dollar a day. Papa did not believe in the divining rod's powers to detect underground flows of water, but Chris Gullard did, so they dug where old Chris's green stick inclined toward the earth.

While they dug, Mamma and I put in a vegetable garden on the acre of plowed ground closest the house—potatoes and turnips and snap beans and cabbages, corn and parsnips and onions, carrots and cucumbers, radishes and beets and lettuce, Hubbard squash and pumpkin and muskmelon. Our mouths watered at the luscious drawings on the seed packages. We had had no green vegetables since last September.

Mamma did not hesitate to prompt God to supply a little more timely moisture to sprout the vegetable seeds, just in case He was looking the other way. Again it rained, not enough to wash out the seeds, but more than enough to swell them and pop them open.

Praise God from Whom all blessings flow!

Meanwhile Papa and Carl buckled down to work with crowbar and pick and shovel and posthole digger to excavate a hole deep enough to permit the six-foot-long iron bit to hang from the short end of a pole balanced over a crotch of stakes set in the ground. This accomplished, Mamma and I could help out. We would shove down on the long end of the pole and then let it go so the sharp wedge of the working end of the plunger would bite into the earth and force the well hole to sink before it. Of course the hole had to be kept primed with water, and it made Papa jump, hauling barrel after barrel from Buffalo Spring and dumping it into what we prayed would eventually be a well close enough for us to enjoy a cold drink whenever we felt like it. What luxury that would be!

If you were lucky, old Chris said, you could strike water up here on the rim at fifteen feet. If you were not, you might go forty, fifty—or you might have to abandon the hole and try another.

We struck water—cold and pure and lots of it—at twenty feet.

When we went to the barn that night to do the chores, Molly had dropped her calf. A beautiful little heifer she was, staggering drunkenly on collapsible legs and butting her mother's swollen bag to bring down the milk. One of the Plymouth Rock hens refused to get off the nest—that meant she was ready to set—and Papa saw the new sickle moon over his right shoulder at dusk.

Next morning, when we opened the door to the rising sun, yet another miracle had been accomplished. The cultivated field, brown yesterday, was now quite definitely green. The wheat and oats were coming up!

There was no doubt about it. God was good. Even the robins were singing His praises from their nests in the buffalo grass.

We were going to stay—not for just fourteen months, but until this thrilling country made us rich and nobody would ever need to work again. We could not do it on a hundred and sixty acres, of course. We'd need more land—like that railroad section east of us that Papa had his eye on. The Northern Pacific was asking ten dollars an acre, but word going around was that they might take as little as four.

Mamma suggested that Papa go to Billings and feel out the bank about a loan, but Papa balked at that. He had always made a habit of paying as he went along and by God he always would. He didn't want to put himself in a position where some skinflint had the right to dun him.

Next thing we knew Uncle Charlie arrived to visit us. Charlie Brown, who was married to Mamma's sister Mamie, was president of the bank in Loyal, Wisconsin. Uncle Charlie was considered well off. He owned his own home as well as a dairy farm outside of Loyal. Without Papa's knowing it, Mamma had written Aunt Mamie that we could pick up a choice piece of land next to us for just about any song we cared to sing; Uncle Charlie ought to take a look at this country anyhow; here was where the future lay. There was more gold to be harvested from the wheat fields than had ever been dug out of the mines.

Uncle Charlie came, saw, and was conquered. He looked at our wheat, six inches tall by then and beginning to ripple in the breeze. He walked across the railroad section—section 33—without a stump on it, and no swamps to drain. That always impressed Easterners. And another thing: there was no danger from cyclones—for as long as the memory of man runneth, there had never been one in Montana. If you had grown up in Wisconsin, where you had to hightail it for the cyclone cellar at least once a year, that was another item not to be sneezed at!

Four dollars an acre, Uncle Charlie mused, looking out across the high flat land of section 33, marred by nothing more serious than an occasional remnant of a buffalo wallow that nature had not had time to erase since the days when the noble bison roamed the high prairie.

"It's a steal," Uncle Charlie said, and then grinned. "But as long as they don't lock us up for the theft, how about stealing it? Say I put up the cash and take title to it. You work it for me, Bob, and we'll go halvers on debt or profit. You can take it off my hands whenever you feel up to it—but each year it will cost you a dollar more per acre. That way my investment's bound to pay me twenty-five percent a year. How does that sound to you?"

It sounded far too good for Papa to resist.

"We'll sow three hundred and twenty acres to winter wheat this fall," Mamma said. "It ought to go around twenty-five bushels to the acre, and that's being conservative. That's roughly eight thousand bushels." (Mamma was a whiz at mental arithmetic.) "Now say we get eighty-five cents a bushel. That's sixty-eight hundred dollars. With half of that ours, we can practically buy the land from you a year from next fall!"

"If the Lord be willin' and the crick don't rise. Amen and hallelujah!" Uncle Charlie chortled. "Jess, I've got to hand it to you. I should've put you to work in the bank instead of advancing you the wherewithal to start that dang millinery store. Anybody who can figure like that . . ."

"Well, show me where I went wrong!"

"You didn't calc'late on expenses," Papa said. "Little items like a gang plow and a tractor to haul it, a seeder, a binder—you take a big chunk of land like section 33, you can't work it with might and muscle and a couple old nags."

"All right, all right," Mamma snapped. It made her mad to have anybody stick pins in her bubbles. "Say *two* years from next fall. We'll let the first three hundred and twenty lie fallow and sow the south half in 1912. Wheat's bound to go up and . . ."

Uncle Charlie's chuckles interrupted her. "You know what you are, Jessie? You're a sketch," he said. "But this time you may be on to something. It won't happen as fast as you hope, but . . ." He turned and stared off to the west. "Look at that damn sky," he said. "It goes on to kingdom come. Why, if I was ten years younger. . ."

Uncle Corve and Aunt Edie came back early in May, pitched a tent and lived in it until the two of them had built a house they could move into. It was bigger and better than ours, but then they had known right from the word Go that they were going to stay. It was a two-hour drive from our homestead to theirs, but we always managed Sunday dinners together, one Sunday at our place on the rim, the next at theirs.

There was plenty for us to do while the crops grew. There was a root cellar to be dug in order to preserve fresh vegetables as long as possible. Milk set in big pans in the cool darkness would not turn sour for a couple days. And someone always had to stay at home to keep stray cattle from getting into the wheat. We needed to fence the whole eight hundred acres, but that would have to wait until we got a hired man. (Thirty dollars a month was the going wage, but a man was usually glad to take fifteen and board during winter months, if you would keep him on. Work was scarce then, and he would have little to do except barnyard chores.) We had no place to sleep a stranger, so Papa started work on a small log bunkhouse in his spare time.

Then there was news of Genevieve's coming early in June. Her romance with Larry Baker seemed to be foundering. Genevieve, now eighteen, wanted to get married right away, but Larry, an honor student in his second year at Madison, had already been tapped by Frank Vanderlip for grooming as a junior executive with the National City Bank in New York provided that Larry maintained his high grades and was graduated with the Magna that so far seemed indicated. Larry was torn between love and a career in the big city, and the career seemed to be winning.

So with Genevieve's visit imminent we would also need another room on the shack. The privacy Mamma and Papa had so far achieved by drawing improvised curtains across the room during the night would no longer serve.

"HE WON'T TAKE A GUN TO US, WILL HE?"

Seven

There was another problem, more pressing than any of the others, Mamma felt: the lack of a school. Now that we were to be wheat ranchers on a grand scale and not merely squatters on a homestead, we must consider What Was Good for the Community as well as our own personal needs.

Not that, selfishly, we did not need a school for me. Mamma would be busier now that we had raised our sights, and it would be impossible for her to continue to give me private lessons. Besides, she told Papa, I would soon be going off to some university—possibly Washington or Stanford—and would require credits for admittance.

"He ain't leaving for a few weeks yet," Papa said.

So, she continued with scarcely a wrinkling of her brow to acknowledge his comment, while she had the time before harvest, she planned to get up a petition and scour the rim for signatures. There was no holding her once she got the bit in her teeth.

Only six children of school age lived within a radius of five miles from the spot Mamma set upon as right and proper for the school. There was Selma Gullard, who had just arrived, the four Torpen kids, and me. To prove that she was not playing favorites, this spot was a mile and a half from our house. It also happened to be on Peterson's land, but that was a minor detail. She caught him when his guard was down—he had been drinking, and drinking even increased his inborn generosity—and he donated the acre before she had finished asking him for it.

Papa saddled up Sam, and Mamma took off with her petition and me on the saddle behind her. We tied Shep to the clothesline to keep him from following.

She bulldozed the indifferent homesteaders into signing her paper. Chris Gullard, of course, was with her. Selma was twelve, and Manda, who was fifteen, might even be able to attend school occasionally when she was not needed to cook and keep house for her father and brothers. The Torpens, with four, signed eagerly, but the others were childless and most of them not yet committed to remaining in Montana.

Perhaps it was because we caught Mrs. Moody with her new store teeth out that she was at first uncooperative. Her two daughters were too old for school anyhow, she said—Kate was fifteen and Edna seventeen—and she intimated that Mamma was getting all these signatures (which would probably only succeed in raising taxes) so *her* daughter, Genevieve, could be hired as the teacher.

Earl Hickson had doubtless spread the word that an eighteen-year-old girl was soon arriving on the rim. "I wish she *would* take the post," Mamma said with a perfectly straight face, "but she won't. She's already been offered a much better position in Billings. So in a year or two your own girls will be old enough to teach—if they have the qualifications."

Mrs. Moody signed.

When we left, I asked Mamma what position Genevieve had been offered in Billings. Mamma frowned. "Did I say that?" she said. "Well, I'm sure she will be offered one."

And even Mr. Kimball signed. He was Mamma's greatest single triumph.

As we came up over the rise behind his shack, we caught the old man hoeing his corn. He spied us too and whisked inside before we could get a good look at him.

"I'm going to *do* it!" Mamma said. "Just you watch me!" She got off the horse, walked up to his door, and knocked. There was no answer. "Mr. Kimball," she said in that now-let's-not-have-any-nonsense tone of hers, "you might as well open the door, because if you don't, I'm going to camp right here. I'm just as stubborn as you are."

Again a long, long wait.

"Very well, Mr. Kimball," she said, sitting down. "You have made your decision; I have made mine." She turned to me. "Get our lunch from the saddlebags, Dale. It's a nice shady place for us to eat."

I unstrapped our lunch, slid off Sam, and dropped the reins on the ground so he would not wander off. Mamma had packed sandwiches and hard-boiled eggs and salt and pickles and marble cake, because we had intended to ride a little farther and picnic in the shade of a tree growing up out of the rim rocks. Mr. Kimball's stoop would serve, however.

"He won't take a gun to us, will he?" I whispered.

"Mr. Kimball wouldn't dare shoot us," Mamma said, very loud. "He is one of God's children—no matter what people may say—and we are God's children, and all we are asking is a signature on a petition to start a school in the wilderness. I'm sure that the uncle of that great actress Clara Kimball Young will be happy to do his part."

We ate our lunch, and presently the door beside us opened, just a crack. I pointed for Mamma to look. She looked, reached for the petition in her handbag, and slipped it through the crack. We never even saw his fingers, but within two minutes the petition reappeared. Mr. Kimball's name was signed in a neat, Spencerian hand.

"Thank you, Mr. Kimball," Mamma said to the closed door. She rose to her feet and brushed the crumbs from her saddle skirt. "When you write that actress niece of yours, please tell her that one of your neighbors enjoyed her acting a few years ago in Chicago."

We could not wait to get home and tell Papa what had happened, but he had news for us too. A hawk had swooped down—while Shep was tied up, thank goodness, so he was not suspect—and carried off one of our chickens.

You could not keep chickens penned up all summer, yet now that the hawk had discovered our flock, something would have to be done or we could lose them all. Chris Gullard told us what he had done last year: he had bought a guinea fowl. A guinea would not fight a hawk or drive it off, but it had telescopic eyesight, combined, apparently, with a higher level of intelligence than the average stupid chicken. A guinea could spot a hawk or an eagle wheeling half a mile in the sky. Then, as it ran for protection, it would emit a blood-curdling, high-pitched trill, which in turn warned the chickens of danger, and the fool hens would leg it for the coop.

Full-grown guineas were scarce and expensive. Papa paid three dollars for a hen on his next trip to Billings, and we almost lost her the moment he turned her loose. Nobody had told him that you had to clip a guinea's wings to keep it from flying away. We watched in horror as she took off. For some reason unknown to the earthbound, she did not immediately head for the horizon but circled and circled above us. "Quick!" Mamma said. "Get some chicken feed."

I ran for a pan of feed and scattered it on the ground. The chickens flocked around, chattering their delight at this untimely meal. And presently the guinea landed among them and began to peck up the grain. She did not try to escape again that whole day and followed the hens into the coop that evening.

Papa and I later found that the chickens had segregated this handsome but different-looking fowl. Though her mission was to save their lives, they pecked at her until she perched alone on the lowest roost.

Papa grabbed her and clipped her wings.

If it had not been for that, no dog could ever have caught her.

I stayed home to watch next day while Mamma went off again with her petition. I wanted to see how the guinea's warning system worked. Along about noon came the shrill sound I had been waiting for. It was a funny thing to

"He Won't Take a Gun to Us, Will He?"

watch. There was the guinea screeching and hot-footing it for the coop, while the chickens first squatted in terror and then followed her, flapping their wings for acceleration. Within seconds the yard was bare of fowl. I squinted up into the blue of the sky and sure enough, there was a hawk that seemed no bigger than a mosquito. He circled for a while and then sailed off.

"By damn, it works!" Papa said. He had come out of the root cellar at the guinea's scream.

"If that's all there is to it," I said, "I bet I could make a noise like that." I tried.

"That's pretty damn good," Papa said. "You could've saved us three dollars—if only your eyes were as good as a guinea's." He laughed and hugged me. "Of course we'd have to stake you out with the chickens every morning, and they got a law against that, so they tell me."

We kept the guinea for a week, and then Shep killed her.

I caught him, as they used to say, with the goods; proud as Punch, he brought me a speckled, slate-colored feather and laid it at my feet.

I was alone at the time. Mamma had one of her sick headaches and was inside the shack with the shades drawn. Papa had gone to Comanche, where, he had been told, he could pick up a safe saddle horse cheap. We needed another horse for a number of reasons. Genevieve would be here shortly and she would like to go for rides, and Mamma would like to have her go. We were buying more cattle, too, so we would need a horse to round them up at night. And when the school was built—Mamma said *when* these days, not *if* —I could ride there in half the time it would take to walk it.

I picked up the feather, and Shep raced ahead to lead me to his prize. He had caught a couple small cottontails before but never attacked a chicken. There was no doubt, however, that the guinea was quite dead. Shep pointed at her, then looked up at me for approval, as if to say: There's not a mark on her.

Papa had said he didn't think Shep was quite bright. He had said, you've got to get rid of a suck-egg dog. Well, this was far worse than sucking eggs. Shep had singled out the most valuable two-legged animal we had and deliberately killed her. I thought I knew why: that hysterical trill of hers had grated on his nerves.

But that would be no excuse to Papa and Mamma.

I was not a liar. I will not say that I never lied, because that would not be the truth, but I had never lied about anything important before. This time, though, it did not even occur to me *not* to lie.

I got the pitchfork and buried the guinea in the manure pile. Then, safely behind the barn, in case Mamma should lift a shade and look out the window of the shack, I practiced the guinea's wierd cry. By placing the tongue in the top of the mouth and trilling over a treble, childish scream, I achieved a startling imitation of the original. At least it fooled Shep, who raced about frantically looking for another guinea, and the chickens stampeded for the protection of the hen house.

It fooled Mamma too. When I went inside, she said the migraine was easing up; lucky the guinea hadn't screamed like that this morning when the pain was at its worst. She couldn't have stood it.

I avoided looking at her and said I guessed the guinea must have spotted a whole herd of hawks. "I think you mean flock," Mamma said. "When they are birds it's flock. Herd is for cattle or buffalo."

Even I forgot the dilemma of the dead guinea hen when Papa came home leading Fly.

"YOU GOT
TO HAND IT
TO THAT GUINEA."

Eight

Fly was a pint-sized, two-year-old chestnut Indian pony. No Black Beauty, my ideal as a horse or almost anything else up to then, she was good-natured and tractable. Already named Fly—because she was small, I suppose—she would come when you called her and lower her head to be scratched behind the ears. She was not the bronco that Papa had gone to get, but once he had seen Fly, he knew he could not be satisfied with the other animal, even though Fly cost ten dollars more. For one thing, the bronco had a sharp spine, and since I would be riding bareback, Fly's round, padded back was far less formidable.

There were fearsome stories about children getting their

feet caught in stirrups and being dragged and trampled to death by frightened animals. A surcingle to hang onto until my legs grew long enough to achieve some leverage was my Papa's solution. If I fell off or was thrown, there would be no damage to anything but pride.

"Will you let Genevieve ride her when she's at home?" Papa asked.

"You mean she's mine?"

Papa nodded.

He lifted me onto Fly's back and led her around for a while. Then I slid off, and he bridled her and fastened the surcingle round her belly. "You've got to learn to get on by yourself," he said. "Let's see." He looked around and spotted a sawhorse. "Lead her up beside that," he said. I did so. "Tell her Whoa when you get her right where you want her."

I said "Whoa," and she stopped. "Now put the reins around her neck—don't ever mount a horse with the reins hanging." I managed that, and Fly stood still for it. Then I climbed onto the sawhorse, and from there it was an easy jump to Fly's back. She nodded and blew her nose in approval, I clucked to her, and she moved off in an easy, bouncy trot. "Hang on!" Papa called, seeing me slipping to one side. "Don't jerk on the bit; neckrein her."

It took time, but Fly was patient and amiable. Finally she eased into a canter, and that was great. No more bouncing, no more hanging on. It was the most exhilarating thing that had ever happened. Suddenly the pony and I were one unit in harmonious motion—free on the limitless prairie. We could go anywhere. I could do anything! I could scream, or laugh, or cry, and there didn't have to be any reason for it.

"Watch out," I heard Mamma yell. "Keep out of my tomato plants!"

The spell was broken. I was once more six years old going on seven, but I found that in the future I could evoke the same release from earth almost at will. The magic ingredients were Fly, a bridle, a surcingle, a sawhorse, and a certain cluck of the tongue. Eventually I didn't even need the sawhorse. Fly would stand still, I would take a run at her from behind (Papa never knew this—he would have been horrified) and vault up over her fat little buttocks onto her back.

That night I was finally about to go to sleep, lulled by Papa's rhythmic snores and the smug thought that I was probably the only six-year-old in the whole world who had a horse of his own, except possibly the Prince of Wales, when I remembered the guinea. That kept me awake a lot longer. My parents had bought me a pony that could run rings around Black Beauty and Ginger, and how had I thanked them? By not confessing what Shep had done to the three-dollar guinea hen.

George Washington, everybody said, could not tell a lie no matter what a larruping his father might give him for telling the truth. But, I reasoned, George had had no such ethical problem as mine. He had cut down a cherry tree—all by himself. It seemed a stupid, pointless thing to do, and he *should* have told the truth about that. If I had killed a guinea hen—it would have been an accident, of course—I'd confess and take the licking too. But I had somebody else to consider: Shep. That complicated the situation.

Since I could not talk to anybody about it, I brought God into the nocturnal discussion. I got out of bed and knelt beside the cot. "God," I whispered—you didn't need to talk very loud to Him, people said; He could even read your lips—"God, You can't really say I told a lie, now can you?" 'There must have been a whole herd of hawks around,' that's all I said. I never said the guinea had seen them. That's the honest-to-God truth, God."

"What are you doing out of bed?" I heard Mamma say.

"Looking for my handkerchief," I said. "I got to blow my nose."

I found the handkerchief and blew lustily, thus retaining my slim franchise on the technicality of not telling a lie. I climbed back into bed but still found sleep elusive. I realized I'd sure better get up at the crack of dawn and let the chickens out of the coop. If Papa beat me to it, he'd miss the guinea.

It rained next day—all day. "It's good for the wheat," Papa said, "and it'll soften up the ground so we can dig postholes."

It was good for me, too. The chickens stayed in the coop. I fed them, cleaned out under the roosts, and gathered the eggs.

The next day was bright and clear. With atmosphere like that, a hawk could spot a prairie dog from five miles in the sky. I let the chickens out and then went into the barn, where Papa was trying to teach the calf to drink out of a bucket. He put his fingers in the calf's mouth, covering its nose with the palm of his hand, and forced its head down into the bucket. She had to breathe somehow, of course, and would suck up some of the milk through her mouth and thus get the idea. "Let me try," I said. I tried, but the calf was stronger than I was and sent me flying galley-west across the barn. "We'll have to put a little more flesh on you," Papa said.

I looked out the barn door and there was Shep hauling the dead guinea out of the manure pile. I slammed the door so Papa wouldn't see, grabbed the thing, threw it back, covered it up once more, and shook my finger in Shep's laughing face. "You leave that there!" I whispered. And then, just to be on the safe side, I let out with the guinea call. The chickens panicked and legged it for the coop, and Shep went crazy looking for another guinea.

When I returned to the barn, the calf was standing, drinking out of the bucket. Papa had to hang onto it for a while because the calf kept bunting the bucket just the way she would bunt her mother's bag to bring down the milk, but in a few days that would be over, and I could feed her.

Papa looked up at me. "You got to hand it to that guinea," he said. "She's a corker when it comes to hawks."

"Yeah," I said, "ain't she?"

Papa took another look at me. "You got a belly ache?" he asked.

"Why?"

"You look like you got a bellyache. Maybe we better give you some castor oil."

"Maybe," I said miserably, "if you think it would do me any good."

While I waited for the evil-tasting stuff to work, I realized how foolish I had been to try to keep the guinea alive. Why hadn't I said that a coyote killed it and carried it off? That would have been so easy, so simple. Of course, it would also have been a deliberate lie, but I might as well face it, by not telling the truth I was just as good—or as bad—as lying. Maybe that's what I'd still better do. It was not too late to blame a coyote, was it?

It didn't much matter whether I lied and went to hell or not as long as I saved Shep from . . . from what? I broke out in sweat all over and hoofed it for the backhouse. If I had not been sick before, I was then—from both ends. Because even if I told the coyote story, what if Shep did not cooperate? What if he dug up that stinking carcass again and brought it to the house?

I must have been bawling, because I did not hear Papa's steps. But suddenly the door opened, and he came in and sat down beside me. After a minute he said, "Shep killed the guinea, didn't he?"

"How do you know?"

"He just dug it out of the manure pile. You buried it there, didn't you?"

I nodded. "He didn't mean to kill it," I said. "It was that racket she made. It made him see red and . . ."

"And you should have told us about it," Papa said. "You know that, don't you?"

"If you want to whip me, go right ahead," I said. "I'll pay you back for the guinea as soon as I'm old enough to hire out."

Papa smiled at that. "It's not the expense," he said. "It's—animals on a farm—they're not just pets. Each one's got to pull its own weight. Now you take the guinea—she had a job to do and she done it. Shep—he don't know what a job is. You'd think he'd have some instinct, but . . . I'm afraid his name is Dennis."

I did not know what that meant, but when Papa said somebody's name was Dennis, well, that put the kibosh on him sure enough.

"Does Mamma know about it?" I asked.

Papa nodded, then he let out a long sigh. "What we

ought to do is get us another dog. You know that as well as I do."

"Yeah," I said, brightening. "If we had another dog for Shep to play around with, then he wouldn't always be getting in Dutch."

Papa shook his head. "I mean . . . give Shep to somebody and get us another dog."

"You *wouldn't!*"

"Damned if I know what we'll do," Papa muttered, looking down at me bawling. "It sure beats me."

What they did was to keep the chickens up until Papa could go to town and buy some chicken wire and then fence them up. It cost money and time that could well have been expended elsewhere, but a hawk would not swoop down inside a small enclosure.

"I'LL PEPPER YOUR TAIL WITH BUCKSHOT!"

Nine

That was the era of the final flowering of unfettered free enterprise in America.

If a man had some gumption in him, if he wasn't afraid to pitch in and get his hands dirty, Papa said, there was no stopping him from achieving any modest goal he might set himself. Papa was a Republican, for practical rather than philosophic reasons. According to him, big mucketymucks like Jim Hill and Jay Gould and the Vanderbilts and the J. P. Morgans (Junior and Senior) would loosen up their purse strings during a Republican administration, and the money would then filter down to the little man.

Democrats, on the other hand, didn't know what was

good for the country. Whenever they got in power, however briefly, they merely succeeded in upsetting the political applecart. They tried to hamstring the big moguls of finance so big business battened down the money hatches and went into hibernation, thus creating a panic until they got back in the saddle under the GOP. Meanwhile, the little man had been wiped out.

The Little Man would always have to knuckle under to the Big Man, no matter what, Papa believed. That's the way the world turned, so face up to it and let the Big Man skim off his cream. It made him feel good, and when a man feels good, he's inclined to be benevolent.

However quaint or cynical such thinking seems today, it was what Papa and a great many men like him believed. If the Democrats were such bogeymen to him, then it is understandable that he saw flaming red at the mere mention of a Wobbly. (The IWW's were not only tolerated by the Democrats, it was said, but actually coddled and encouraged for their votes.)

God help the world in general, people said, if the Wobblies were its International Workers. (Even to mention the sturdy and venerable word *workers* in connection with those lazy bums was ridiculous; everybody knew IWW really stood for I Won't Work.) And God help the poor farmer who found himself at the mercy of a Wobbly in an emergency. The Wobbly might be barefoot and in rags, the legend went, his hair might be crawling with fleas, and he might not have a dime in his pockets or know where his next can of beans was coming from, but he always had a watch. When he pulled it out and looked at it, and the short hand pointed to five and the long to twelve, it was quitting time, even if he was right in the middle of milking a cow or had not yet unhitched his team from a binder. He just quit and walked away.

It was the first of June. The root cellar was roofed and sodded over, a bedroom added to the shack, and the bunkhouse ready for the hired man we so badly needed to help with the building of the fences. As if on signal, Rudy Bristow walked in on us. He had heard from Mr. Robinson in Acton that we needed a man and that we, like most of the folks up on the rim, were from Wisconsin. Rudy was from Wisconsin himself, he said. Baraboo, to be exact.

Well, Papa had once been in Baraboo. In fact, there was almost nowhere in Wisconsin that he had not been, and any man from anywhere in the Badger State needed no further recommendation. Rudy Bristow was from Baraboo, Wisconsin; therefore he was fair and square. Providence, through the agency of Charlie Robinson, had obviously sent him to us.

Rudy was about thirty-five, sandy-complexioned, and cadaverous. He was, he remarked during supper that first evening, quite a reader, and he asked if he might borrow the copy of *Silas Marner* he noticed on a shelf in our Globe Werniecke bookcase. He liked to peruse a few pages before putting out the lamp. It made him drowsy.

Mamma was delighted to lend it to him. Literacy among the working classes was to be encouraged. But Papa said afterward that he should have smelled a mouse right then and there. What kind of fancy talk was that *peruse* stuff? A man who did a good, honest day's work did not need a book to *peruse* to put him to sleep.

Papa had to wake Rudy up next morning. He had slept the sleep of the just, he said, for the first time in many moons. Perhaps it was merely being with folks from back home after all this time, his kind of folks. Or maybe it was hoofing it for ten miles the day before.

He ate a dozen pancakes smothered in maple syrup (which Aunt Mamie and Uncle Charlie had sent us from the spring rising of their sugar bush) , three eggs, and six slices of bacon, before he paused for breath. The last outfit he worked for, he explained, was a big cattle ranch out of Ryegate, and they had a Chinaman to cook grub for the hands. The little yellow man was not bad as little yellow men go, but give Rudy good American home cooking three times a day every day in the week, he said, letting his belt out two notches.

Mamma said it did her heart good to see a man enjoy his victuals.

"A man's got to stoke his furnace or he can't do an honest day's work," Papa said. "Pitch right in."

"I don't mind if I do," said Rudy, and reached for four more pancakes.

Fence posts were free. All you had to do was drive to the north rim, chop down cedar of the proper girth, strip it of branches and bark, crosscut-saw it into five-foot lengths, load it onto the wagon, and then distribute it at twenty-five-foot intervals along the boundary of your property.

Rudy lasted two days and then came down with what he surmised darkly must be Rocky Mountain spotted fever. It was not dangerous, he said, but damned uncomfortable while it lasted. And how long might it last, Papa asked? That all depended, Rudy said, but, well, there was nothing for it but to go to bed and keep quiet. Keep quiet and eat, eat hearty, even if you had to force yourself, that's what he had been told. Otherwise you would lose strength and vitality, and the fever might lay you low for months on end.

Mamma plied him with food and tried to think of things that would tempt the poor, sick man's appetite. She would carry his meals to the bunkhouse, knock on the door, leave the food on the step, and then hurry away. (The fever was only transmitted by the bite of a wood tick, Rudy said, but still and all there was no point in taking chances with anything so painful.) Half an hour later she would return and find the empty dishes stacked neatly outside the bunkhouse door. Once *Silas Marner* was laid beside the dishes with a note asking if he could borrow the Bible.

A week passed. Mamma began to entertain doubts. "You know what I think?" she said to Papa one morning. "I'll bet if you were to go to the bunkhouse and tell Rudy you were through chopping trees, his fever would cure right up."

"Now, Jessie," Papa said. "A man from Baraboo, he wouldn't pull a stunt like that."

"Well, I'm from Missouri," Mamma snorted, "and you've got to show me!" (She was *not* from Missouri, of course. That was merely something you said when you were skeptical.)

Mamma began to cut down on the portions she carried to the bunkhouse. Papa let it go for a couple more days but you could see that he was beginning to fume. He was a good, simple man, but there was one thing that would rouse him to fury: his trust and goodwill being taken advantage of.

It was now the middle of June and next day we were going to Acton to meet Genevieve. That evening after supper Papa walked to the bunkhouse, went inside, and closed the door after him. A few minutes later the door flew open and through it hurtled the lean and hungry body of Rudy Bristow. Right behind him came his telescope bag and his hat. Then Papa stood in the doorway dusting his hands.

"You show yourself around here again and I'll pepper your tail with buckshot!" Papa yelled.

Rudy picked up his bag and his hat and high-tailed it off toward Comanche.

"Your mamma was right," Papa said. Shep and I had been hiding behind the bunkhouse so as not to miss any of the fireworks. "I felt of his forehead—it was as cool as a bullsnake—before I let him have it," Papa went on.

We stood and watched Rudy grow smaller and smaller in the sunset. "I can't get over it," Papa said, scowling. "A four-flusher like that from Baraboo, Wisconsin!" Then he brightened a little. "There's just one way to account for it. He must've joined up with the IWW's."

"Did you ever see his watch?" I asked.

Papa shook his head. "No, but he probably had to pawn it to get down here from Ryegate." He turned back into the bunkhouse. It smelled like a rabbit warren in there, he said. He'd have to fumigate. "Peruse," he muttered. "I should've known."

There was only one good thing about the episode with Rudy: if Papa had not kicked him out that day, we would never have brought Jim Harper home along with Genevieve.

"SEEMS LIKE IT'S A MILLION MILES FROM NOWHERE."

Ten

Mamma and I drove to Acton to meet Genevieve next morning. Papa was digging postholes so he would not need Sam and Babe.

The train from Billings was late. While we waited, a good-looking young man ambled into the little depot. He was seventeen years old and carried a .22 and a battered grip. He had noticed our team and figured somebody must be meeting somebody today, therefore the train would stop and he could board it without a fuss. A conductor, he had learned from experience, was liable to get sore as a boiled owl if his train was flagged down to pick up a passenger going no more than fifty cents' worth up the line, and fifty cents' worth was all the farther he could afford to go that day.

He spoke with an accent I had heard only once before. Our porter on the train from St. Paul talked like that. "What part of the South are you from, young man?" Mamma asked.

"Virginia, ma'am?" he said. "Culpeppeh County?" The way his voice rose at the end of each remark made it sound as if he was asking our approval of what he had said. If we did not think well of his coming from Culpepper County, then he would be happy to oblige us by coming from somewhere else.

"My father was in Virginia during the war," Mamma said. "With Grant."

"That's nice," the boy said.

And where was he headed?

Farther west. No particular destination, though before he turned around and started back—if he ever did—he'd sure like to take a gander at the Pacific Ocean. He had been working for a certain individual near Glendive, but they couldn't hit it off. "It was most likely my fault, ma'am, but seemed like to me he was a mean ole customer," he said. So he collected his pay and bought himself a ticket for as far as it would take him, which was Acton. Well, he got off the train yesterday and looked around and just couldn't seem to cotton to it. "Seems like it's a million miles from nowhere," he said.

"Where did you sleep last night," Mamma asked.

"Under a culvert, ma'am."

I could see that Mamma liked him. She looked him up and down. His clothes were cheap, but they were neat and clean. We heard the train whistle in the distance. "Do you

"Seems Like It's a Million Miles from Nowhere."

mind if I ask you a personal question?" Mamma said. She seemed to be in a hurry.

"Shucks no, ma'am," he said, "you jus' ask away to your heart's content."

"Why did you leave home?"

"I didn't rightly leave home, ma'am," he said. "I ran off from the orphanage when I was fourteen."

"You poor boy," Mamma said. She turned and looked off down the track. The train was in sight. "How would you like to come and work for us? Our place is up on the rim and there's one thing you can say for it: it's a lot closer to nowhere than this. We need a man—bad."

"I don't know as you could call me a man yet awhile, but I reckon I will be pretty soon," he said. "Of course I wouldn't want to hire out to you without you knowing it was temporary."

"You're open and aboveboard," Mamma said. "The pay is thirty dollars a month during summer and fall."

"Okay, then," he said. "It's a sure enough deal."

"Our name is Eunson," Mamma said.

"Is that . . . Scandinavian?" the boy asked.

"No, it's Scottish. And while it is spelled E-U-N-S-O-N, we pronounce it *Unson.*"

"That's nice," he said. "My name's Harper. At least that's the handle they gave me at the orphanage. Jim Harper."

Genevieve was probably the prettiest sister any boy ever had. She had just passed her eighteenth birthday, and though that made her only a year older than Jim Harper, she was a young woman and he was still a boy.

She had a mop of long, wavy, chestnut hair, which she

washed twice a week in water from the rain barrel, rinsed with vinegar, and dried and brushed in the sun until it was soft and shiny as satin. If she was going to stay at home, she wore it in a braid bigger than my arm, but when she had a date to go riding with a young man, she would pile it and tease it into a pompadour and then dazzle it—and her young man—with silk ribbons.

She and Mamma seemed to try to make a fresh start together. Success, both of them sensed intuitively, was a possibility, but only with a bare minimum of contact. When Mamma was cooking, Genevieve would manage to be out hoeing and weeding the garden. And when Genevieve chose to make fudge or penuche, or play and sing the new songs she had brought with her, Mamma could find things to do like churning out on the stoop or skimming the milk and candling the eggs in the gloom of the root cellar. Or sometimes I would see her turn quite pink in the face and then rush outside to fan herself with her apron. "Whew, it's hot!" she would say.

When we were all together, Mamma would sometimes stare out the window the way the prisoners used to in the jail cells back in Neillsville. She would let out audible sighs, and I would catch Genevieve looking at her as if to say: You can't make me lose my temper. This is my home as much as it is yours until I get married; if I have to leave it, Papa's going to know whose fault it is.

It made the situation no more endurable for Mamma to find Genevieve such a magnet. Young men rode in from as far off as Broadview. There were sons of farmers and a clerk from the feed store and a demonstrator for milk separators, Harry Gullard and a cowhand from out west of Comanche, and Earl Hickson. It was funny how they would just happen to be out hunting and passing by the Eunsons of a Sunday afternoon. Will Murphy resorted to no such obvious dodge. He came down all the way from Judith Gap, where he ran a drugstore, with the avowed purpose of paying court. Genevieve had met him on the train that day between Billings and Acton. They had known each other for less than an hour, but that hour left him totally bemused.

Sometimes there were two or three young swains at a time. They would crowd into the shack, the tall ones like Harry and Will stooping to get through the door. Genevieve would ply them with candy and cake and hot chocolate and marshmallows (which she made herself), and then Shep would be banished because he howled, and she would sit down at the piano.

The boys would gather round, and she would play them the new ragtime songs she had brought along—"Maple Leaf Rag" and "Some of These Days"—and then they would go back to the old ones they knew and loved like "Redwing" and "Pony Boy" and "Put on Your Old Grey Bonnet" (which always made Papa blow his nose vigorously). Then like as not somebody would ask Papa to do a jig, and he'd say, "Hell, I can't dance any more, I got this damn rheumatiz," but he was getting to his feet as he said it, and Genevieve would strike up "The Irish Washerwoman." His rheumatiz would miraculously desert him and he would proceed to shake the shack with a real old hoedown.

Somehow Mamma felt left out of all this. She would turn pink and then take me by the hand and lead me out onto the stoop, where there was a rocking chair. "What's the matter, Mamma?" I'd say, and she'd say, "Nothing," and blink her eyes as if to keep from crying. "There're just too many people in there on such a hot day. It's stuffy."

"I wish you liked Genevieve, Mamma," I said once.

"*I* like Genevieve," she said. "It's Genevieve who doesn't like me."

None of the boys had ever seen anything quite like my sister, at least not on the prairie of Montana. They all wanted to marry her, and I think Will Murphy had the inside track for a while, but she accepted nobody and turned nobody down. She needed time to think, I heard her tell Will one day as they returned from a ride over to the haunted house on the edge of the rim.

This was not merely a female gambit to keep them all on the string. Oh, it was probably that too, but she did need time to think, because she was still corresponding with Larry Baker. Nobody had to prompt her to ride Fly down to Acton for the mail every day or so. I suspect now that she was beginning to question her stubborn refusal to wait for Larry, but she had said she would not, and now she could not take it back.

We had fresh green onions and radishes on the table at last. The string beans and peas were dutifully mounting their shaky twine trellises, and the cucumber, squash, and pumpkin vines were sprouting runners. The potato and tomato plants were in blossom, and there were actually ears on the cornstalks, ears with the silk beginning to show! (Well, not actually *show*; I had to peel back the husk a little to find it.)

In the field past the garden the wheat stood a foot high, and the hot sun drew it higher every day. Papa and Jim hurried with the fencing because the Reynolds cattle still ranged the prairie and much preferred the succulent young domestic crop to the tough buffalo grass. Let fifty longhorns onto a forty-acre tract, and you'd have no problem about a harvest, Chris Gullard said. That was, of course, a joke.

But we ran in luck that year. The only marauder was a bear.

While Genevieve was with us, I shared the bunkhouse at night with Jim. He climbed into the top bunk, and I took the lower, so Shep could get in bed with me if he wanted to. Mamma gave Jim our old magazines—the *Saturday Evening Post* and *St. Nicholas* and the *National Geographic*—but I noted that he seldom cracked them. He liked *Judge* and *Captain Billy's WhizBang,* which he kept on a shelf so high I couldn't reach it.

But after the lamp was out, I would get Jim to telling stories about the things he had done and the places he'd been. I suppose Jim was a born liar, but his yarns made fascinating listening for a not-quite-seven-year-old who believed every detail.

He had a hairbreadth escape from a truant officer who was looking for him in Appomattox, for instance. Jim sensibly hid under a culvert. The only trouble was, it rained and the water rose fast. Jim would always pause at this point to roll himself a cigarette and light it in the dark, and I would obligingly prompt him. "What did you do then, Jim?" I would ask, holding my breath.

"You really want to know?" he'd ask, teasing me.

Well, he'd go on, the miserable old truant officer was still snooping around, so Jim didn't dare crawl out just yet awhile, and then finally the water rose, and danged if it didn't flush him right out of the culvert like a steer coming out of a chute, but he grabbed aholt of an old torn piece of tarp that was hanging there on a oleander bush just outside the culvert, and he covered himself with it and floated down the gully right under the eyes of the mean old villain who was fixin' to pick him up and carry him back to the orphanage.

"Gosh," I'd say, "not at Appomattox where Robert E. Lee surrendered to General Grant?"

"The very same," Jim would say. "Now go to sleep."

Looking back on it, I realize that Jim's adventures had a suspicious pattern: they always took place in familiar locales. There was the time he was lost for three days in Mammoth Cave and lived on mushrooms, and—riding the rails and legends west—the time he was drugged and rolled in a saloon in Deadwood.

Still, I like to think they all happened, and maybe they did. Certainly if he ever told the episode of the bear later, that was true. I could vouch for it.

Shep woke me. He was whimpering and scratching at the door to the bunkhouse. It was not yet daylight; there was nothing but a golden glow to the East. I opened the door and Shep bolted out barking his head off. There stood a brown bear in the vegetable patch, peeling the husks off a tender ear of corn. He had apparently intended to cross the table of the rim during the night, but the tantalizing odors from our garden had seduced him.

The bear saw Shep charging toward him and ambled off. The way he moved, he could easily outrun Shep if he wanted to.

"Jim! Git your .22!" I yelled.

Jim slept in his union suit. He staggered to his feet and looked out the door. "By God," he said, "if it ain't a bear!"

He didn't bother to pull on his pants, just grabbed up his .22 and made for the barn. In a shorter time than it takes to tell, he had Fly outside, had her bridled, and was on her bare back tearing out across the wheat field after the bear and Shep. The last I saw of them as they disappeared over the rise, the bear was leading Shep by a hundred yards and gaining.

Mamma and Papa and Genevieve had all been awakened by the disturbance, and I told them proudly that it was Shep and I who had discovered the bear. I took them out to the garden to show them just where. Sure enough, there were the tracks—big ones, too.

We heard a shot.

A couple minutes later Shep came loping back over the rise, his tail between his legs. He approached us apologetically, sat on his haunches, and offered his paw as he always did when he thought he was in trouble.

"Look at his nose," Papa said. "It's all bloody."

There was a gash across his nose. Apparently, once out of sight of the house and before Jim could catch up with them the bear had stopped, waited, and given Shep a nasty slash with his paw.

After a little while Fly came trotting back with Jim, who looked happy and excited, not realizing until he started to dismount that he still wore nothing but his union suit. He settled down on Fly's back once more. He had got the damn bear right through the noggin with one shot, he boasted.

"You were plumb lucky, with nothing but a .22," Papa said. "If I'd been there, I wouldn't have let you take a crack at him thataway. You might've just nicked him, and he could've turned on you, and then you'd've been up the crick!"

"Ain't that a fact?" Jim said, realizing it for the first time. Somehow I have the feeling now that when he told the story to some other lucky kid later, he *did* just nick the bear, and the bear turned on him and—but Jim would embroider it much better than I could.

He and Papa skinned the bear and salted down the hide and head until Jim had time to take it to a taxidermist in Billings. It was gone for several months. When it finally came back—an awesome thing six-feet-nine from snarling mouth to modest tail, and lined in fiery red felt—Jim offered it to Mamma. The bear had been killed on our property, and he suspected it belonged to us anyhow, he said, especially since Papa had plunked down thirty-five bucks for the curing and mounting.

Mamma thanked Jim, but declined. Legally the bearskin might be ours, she admitted, but it was not so much a question of what was legal and what was not, but where would she put it? Walking over to the table from the stove with a bowl of hot soup, she might inadvertently put her foot in the bear's open mouth, trip, and make a terrible mess. She would much rather for Jim to keep it in the bunkhouse where it would cover the cracks in the floor and be nice and warm to his feet when he stepped out of bed on a cold morning.

Besides, she confided to Papa while Jim happily lugged the bearskin to his private domain, it would be a good influence on a boy to have something more than a .22 to take pride in and call his own. It might settle him down.

"STALLIONS THAT DANCED ON GOLDEN HOOVES"

Eleven

Earl Hickson had invited Genevieve to go to the roundup in Billings on the fourteenth of August. (I remember well because the fifteenth would be my seventh birthday, and that was what started the trouble.) They had been going to ride horseback—that would be much faster—but Mamma pointed out sensibly (Genevieve herself had to admit it) that even a girl as pretty as she would look dusty and bedraggled after jouncing for twenty miles on the back of a sweaty horse. So why didn't they take our buggy?

Papa had recently bought us one to use when we drove over to visit Aunt Edie and Uncle Corve. It had springs front and rear and a top that protected Mamma's fair skin from the sun. "You're welcome to it," Papa said.

Genevieve was undecided, probably because she did not know how to accept a suggestion of Mamma's gracefully. It was up to Earl, she finally said. Earl, who liked Mamma very much, said it was a dandy idea.

So it was settled. Mamma got into the swing of things and insisted upon retrimming Genevieve's hat. When it was finished, Genevieve tried it on and looked at herself in the mirror over the washbasin outdoors. She could not help knowing how flattering it was. She turned and mumbled something that sounded like "Thank you, Mother," but I could not be sure of that last word.

Earl had been to the roundup last summer and told us all about it. It was held in a field north of Billings at Twenty-eighth Street and Twelfth Avenue. There were saddleback and bareback races and bronco busting. There was competitive bulldozing of steers, and there was trick riding. The Crow Indians would swarm in off the reservation in droves and demonstrate on some hapless steer how they used to kill buffalo. (The steer was later barbecued.) Sometimes they even reenacted their triumph over Custer, but that made the townspeople a little nervous. When Indians got to whooping it up like that, they said, the Lord only knew where it would end.

But what electrified me was Earl's mention of the two stars and masters of ceremonies of the roundup: the brother-and-sister team of Jack and Lucille Mulhall. They led the grand parade on coal-black Arabian stallions that danced on golden hooves!

Golden hooves! I had never dreamed of a horse dancing—and on Golden Hooves to boot! It sounded like something out of the Land of Oz—only better, because everything in Oz was green. "Can't I go, Mamma?" I asked, when I found her alone in the shack putting up green-tomato pickles.

It was blistering hot that day. The heat had not broken for a week, and the black tarpaper of the shack made a furnace out of it, a furnace redolent today of vinegar and mustard and cloves and pickling spices. Sweat poured off Mamma's face as she stirred the pickles on the back of the range. She stopped and wiped her eyes with her apron, then looked out the window to where Earl was telling Genevieve that if Papa did not mind what time he got her home, he could take her to the Northern Hotel dining room for supper after the roundup. That was the swellest hotel in town; why, even the Mulhalls put up there.

"You could ask your father," Mamma said after a while.

Papa and Jim were stringing and stretching wire on the fence at the southwest corner of section 33, but Shep and I ran the distance in fifteen minutes flat. When I could stop puffing I told them about the stallions with golden hooves and how much I wanted to see them. "Mamma must think it's all right," I said. "She could have said no right then if she didn't. She said ask you."

Papa squatted down on his haunches and set me on one of his knees. He said he was going to have to say no, and he did not expect me to understand, but Earl had not asked me, he had asked Genevieve.

"He probably just forgot," I said.

Papa shook his head and smiled at Jim. "No, I don't expect he forgot. Do you, Jim?"

"I reckon not," Jim answered. Then he turned to me. "You be thinkin' 'bout somethin' else you'd choose to do on that day, and we'll do it," he said. "Say! How 'bout me buyin' some yellow paint next time I go to town, and we'll paint ole Fly's hoofs?"

I tried to imagine fat little Fly with yellow feet, but there was no magic in the vision.

The morning of the fourteenth the sun rose a little before five o'clock. Jim was already up, probably milking, when I woke and walked to the door of the bunkhouse. It was going to be a scorcher. You could already feel the heat of the sun. Black smoke poured out of the stovepipe in the shack. That meant Mamma had just started the fire; breakfast would not be ready yet awhile.

Shep was nowhere in sight. A movement up in the wheat field caught my eye. It was Papa out for a morning stroll. Shep was probably with him, but the wheat was so tall it hid him. It had long since headed out, and the green had turned to gold except for a few dark blotches in what had been the richer land around the buffalo wallows. That took longer to ripen.

Papa liked to pick a few heads of wheat every day and rub the kernels between his fingers. That's how you could tell when it was time to harvest. You did not want to cut and bind too soon-if the kernels were still moist they'd shrink and lose weight—but on the other hand you didn't dare wait too long. If the heads got too ripe, part of the grain was liable to shell out when the binder hit it.

I did not feel very well and climbed back into the bunk. After a while Mamma came looking for me. She felt my forehead. There was apparently no fever. She wanted to know if I felt queasy. I did not. Then what was wrong? Where did I feel bad?

Not in any particular place, I said. I just felt sort of

droopy all over and thought I'd stay in bed until after Earl and Genevieve got started.

"I see," Mamma said. Then she made a thin line out of her lips. "Certain people," she said, "are very selfish."

"Who, Mamma?"

"Never mind who."

She got up off the bunk where she had been sitting and hit her head on Jim's upper bunk. It staggered her for a minute. She scowled and rubbed her head, then walked to the door and stared outside. I could hear Earl's horse galloping down the road. After a little while she turned around. "How would you like to go see those stallions with golden hooves for your birthday present?"

"But Papa said I couldn't."

"You leave Papa to me," she said, slapping her hands together. Then she turned back to the open door and spoke, as if she were talking to Papa, "There's no good reason on God's green earth why he shouldn't go along if he wants to that much."

"Oh, Mamma!" I said. "How're you going to put it across with Genevieve?"

Genevieve was to know nothing about it, Mamma said, until it was too late. While Mamma put breakfast on the table for everybody—Earl would probably have a bite too; he always seemed to have room whether he had eaten before or not—she would tell them I was staying in bed for a while because I had a stomach ache. Then, while they were eating, I was to get dressed and run down to the shed where we kept the buggy and crawl in under the seat—it was a small space, but I was small enough for it—and hide.

"Till when, Mamma?" I whispered.

"You better keep undercover till you get past Holdup Hill," she said. "That'll be too far for them to turn around and bring you home."

"I'll bet they'll be mad as a wet hen," I said.

"Oh, pshaw," she said. "It'll be a good joke on them."

The plan would probably have worked if it had not been for Shep. Not more than a mile from the house, Genevieve looked around and saw him trotting along behind. Earl stopped and told him to go home. Shep simply stood and looked at them. Earl got out of the buggy and made threatening gestures. Shep ran around in front, sat down, and peered at Earl between the horse's legs.

"I don't understand it," I heard Genevieve say. "He never followed me before except once when I went to Acton and Dale rode behind me on Fly."

There was a long silence, and the next thing I knew Earl had lifted the flap over my hiding place and was staring down at me. "Well, look what we have here," he said. "A stowaway."

Earl and Genevieve were not really mad at me at all. It seemed as if they thought it was what any normal kid would do. Genevieve remarked that she had been kind of worried about me because I *didn't* get in more trouble. It was unnatural for a boy to be so tractable, so she was glad to see me try to pull a stunt like this. It showed I was a real boy. But of course I could not go along. They would not be home until all hours tonight, and the folks would be worried.

"No, they won't," I said. "I've been out till all hours lots of times."

For some reason Earl laughed at that. He said, "How about it, Gen? Shall we take him? I imagine the folks would soon catch on to where he was."

"Catch on," I said, "they already know. At least Mamma knows, and she's sure to tell Papa before he gets to worrying."

Genevieve got a very strange look on her face. "So Jessie put you up to this," she said. "I might have known it."

By the time we got back to the shack, Papa and Jim had taken Fly over to be serviced by Ed Ives's stud horse. Mamma was alone. She had finished the dishes and was setting a batch of bread. Sweat poured off her face, and her hands were sticky with dough when Genevieve led me in the door.

"Well, what's this?" she said. "Did you forget something?"

"No," Genevieve said. "We did not forget a thing. We found we had something we had not expected, that's all."

"What is it?"

That was a mistake, of course. If Mamma had not pretended total ignorance of the plot, I suspect Genevieve might have let it go. Instead she had to ask, "What is it?"

Well, you had to hand it to Mamma sometimes. Catch her red-handed with the plans for blowing up the U.S. mint and she would maintain with her last breath before a firing squad that it was merely Grandma Romaine's recipe for piccalilli. And what's more, she would convince herself it was true.

"You know very well what it is," Genevieve said angrily. "Dale? Why, I thought you loved your little brother," Mamma said, "and since tomorrow's his birthday, it would be a nice thing for you to do for him."

"I'm going to buy him a birthday present," Genevieve said, and turned on me still in the same angry tone. "Tell me what you want."

"I don't want anything—from *you*!" I said. I was mad at them both. Mamma put her floury arms around me as if to comfort me, but I did not feel comforted. Does a pawn ever feel comforted when he is deliberately sacrificed?

"Well, of course," Mamma said, "it just never occurred to me that you and Earl would be up to anything you wouldn't want Dale to report to your father later."

Genevieve's mouth dropped open. She spluttered, started to say something, then thought better of it and hurried out of the shack, letting the screen door slam behind her. Mamma winced—she hated for anyone to slam doors—and her eyes looked after Genevieve for quite a spell. We heard the buggy wheels crunch in the gravel. Finally Mamma glanced down at her hands. "Goodness Godness Agnes!" she exclaimed. "I better stop twiddling my thumbs and get this bread set. Why don't you practice your five-finger exercises?"

I did not feel like practicing my five-finger exercises, I told her. It was too hot.

"Well, I don't care what you do," she said, "but do *something!*"

Mamma was always saying that. This time I asked her why.

"Because," she said without a moment's pause, "nature abhors a vacuum."

"Oh," I said, and went outside, being careful not to let the screen door slam.

Jim had made me a pair of stilts and during that summer I seldom even went to the privy without them. Starting me out with the steps nailed to the poles no more than six inches from the base, he had raised them a little at a time until, as I grew adept at walking, they were now two feet off the ground. Higher than that, he said, they could be dangerous. I could take a nasty fall if I lost my balance.

The stilts leaned against the side of the house and I climbed onto them now, tucked the poles under my arms, and moved off up the rise. I took gizzard-jarring, giant steps and tried not to think how much I hated my sister and Mamma and even Shep, because he had betrayed me. But it was wicked to hate, so I wished I was dead and then everybody would be sorry and wonder why they hadn't been nicer to me while they had the chance. I might be dead, too, I thought. I could fall off my stilts and hit my head on a rock any minute now.

I fantasized myself laid out in the coffin with my hands folded—I had once been taken to a funeral back in Neillsville and it had made an indelible impression—and the scar from the rock still there on my forehead. Everybody was gathered around, Mamma and Genevieve crying the hardest, and Papa saying to Genevieve, "Why didn't you let him go with you? He would be with us now if you had."

Shep was there in the fantasy too, lying right alongside me. He howled when they began to sing "Abide with Me," and somebody grabbed him and started to put him out, but I raised up in my coffin and made them let him loose. If he wanted to howl, he could howl!

I was crying, so I had to get down off my stilts. Stilts were not made to cry on. Shep licked my face sympathetically, and I let him until I remembered that if it hadn't been for him I'd be four or five miles down the road toward the dancing stallions with the golden hooves by now. I shoved him away from me and stared off toward the western horizon.

Comanche was upside down, shimmering in an emerald sea. A Great Northern freight rolling south from Broadview ran right into the water and disappeared for a while, then reappeared farther south. It too was inverted like Comanche, the smoke from the big mogul locomotive falling instead of rising. A plume of white steam indicated a whistle for the crossing at Comanche. I began to count slowly: One stick-in-the-mud, two stick-in-the-mud, three stick-in-the-mud-until I got to thirty-one and the crazy freight had left Comanche far behind. Then the faint sad wail of the whistle made Shep prick up his ears.

I stared at the train for as long as I could see it, till I felt dizzy and the waves of the sea commenced to lap against the shore where Buffalo Spring ought to be. Then I heard Papa's voice. "What are you doing way up here?"

He and Jim were bringing Fly back from Ed Ives's place. "Nothing," I said. "But look at that flood."

It was not a flood, Papa said, just a mirage, but the damnedest mirage he ever hoped to see. "It's the heat," he said, removing his hat and wiping his forehead with his sleeve. "Looks like it might break, though. See that cloud?"

Way past Broadview, even way past Oz, a radiant white picture-book cloud was pasted on the aqua vault of the sky. It seemed to have been sheared off in a sharp gray line about a mile above the horizon, and looked as if the sun was drawing water out of the mirage and replenishing the cloud with it. A gray and white curtain suspended from the cloud swept the distant prairie.

"I declare, I never seen one quite like that," Jim said. "You reckon that don't hold a cyclone?"

"If this was Wisconsin I'd say it did, sure as Billy-be-damned," Papa said. "But anyways, no need for us to worry. That'll pass way north of us."

"NOBODY COULD HEAR ANYTHING BUT THE HAIL."

Twelve

Jim's eyes swept the horizon. "Seems like there's another one abuildin' over there past Molt," he said.

Papa looked off to the left. "Could be," he said. The heat today had erased all except a few faint stains of green among the gold in the wheat. "Well, as long as it rains gentle," he said. "But if it's cats and dogs, that's God's will, and there ain't a damn thing we can do about it except collect the kittens and the pups."

"That's about the size of it," Jim said.

I looked speculatively at Fly. "Is she going to have a colt?"

"Ask me that in a few months," Papa said. "That's part of God's puzzle too."

"When people get to jawing at each other, is that part of God's puzzle too?"

Papa looked at Jim and shrugged. "Search me," he said. "Here. Give me your foot. I'll help you up on Fly."

"I got my stilts," I said. I climbed onto them and stomped along beside Papa and Jim. "Lookit," I said, "I'm taller'n you are."

But only for a moment. I failed to see a gopher hole, jammed a stilt into it and took a header. Papa picked me up off the ground and offered to carry me the rest of the way because I had knocked a tooth loose and my mouth was bleeding. It hurt like the old Harry, but I could neither cry nor let Papa carry me in front of Jim, much as I would have liked it. I walked along beside them, blinking back the tears and leaning forward to keep from bloodying my shirt and knickers.

Mamma was not very sympathetic. It was about time the tooth came out anyhow, she said, and she had a painless method for pulling it: tie one end of a string around the tooth and the other to the flatiron, then drop the iron. I needn't do it right away if I was scared. I could hold the iron in my lap for as long as I wanted to, or even carry it with me if I had to go to the privy. But eventually I would forget, make a sudden move, and the weight of the iron would yank the tooth out. I would hardly notice it, she declared.

I sat in the rocking chair out on the stoop, holding the flatiron in my lap. When that got tiresome, I carefully set it on the floor and bent over so that the string would remain slack and put no strain on the loose tooth. Mamma tried to trick me by calling and asking me to bring in some wood—she had to keep a fire going in the range because the bread was baking—but I was too smart to be taken in by such an obvious ruse. I merely lugged the iron along with me.

Then she reminded me that I had not done my practicing. There she thought she had me, but she was mistaken. I set the flatiron on the music rack beside Czerny and went to work.

The fresh bread came out of the oven. The odor made my mouth water. I could have a piece—with butter and brown sugar, just the way I liked it—but not until I stopped being silly and dropped the flatiron.

I stared hungrily at the bread as Mamma cut and buttered a slice for herself. "I think it's turning a bit cooler," she said.

The windows were all open. I could hear the calf bawling—she was hungry all the time—and the chickens caw-cawing, grumbling about the heat. I thought I heard another sound too; it was like the distant rumble of a train. Only when the atmosphere was just right, usually on cold, clear winter nights, could we hear anything except the whistle of trains. Maybe, I thought, this was an unusually long freight, and I went back to Czerny. Half an hour of Mr. Czerny, and then I could practice "Fireflies."

Shep came to the screen door and scratched to be let in. Mamma paid no attention. It was still too hot to have a dog in the house. He began to whine. "Can I go play with Shep for a while?" I asked. "I'll come in and practice when it's cooler."

"You can do anything you want to," Mamma said, "if you'll drop that flatiron. I'm sick of seeing you drooling around that string."

That meant I could not go out and play until I pulled my tooth. It wasn't fair, I thought. First she said I could take my own sweet time about it, and now I was being punished until I dropped the flatiron. I sat on the piano stool and sulked.

Mamma went to the door. "I'm going to pick us some roasting ears for supper. Why don't you come along and we'll see if the new potatoes are big enough for a few helpings?"

That was a fierce temptation, and she knew it. I had been wanting to pull a potato bush for several weeks to take a look, but she said she could tell by the tops that the spuds weren't ready yet, and of course once you disturbed a potato bush, you couldn't put it back.

I shook my head. Mamma shrugged, opened the door, and went out. Shep, who had been whining, slithered through the opening and made it inside. Mamma saw him and told him to get out. She probably thought in the confusion I would drop the flatiron and that would be that.

But Shep came to me and put his paws in my lap as if he was afraid of something. The shack was still except for that train that kept coming, closer now. It must be the longest darn train in the whole world, I thought.

A sudden gust of wind billowed the west curtains into the room and flattened the east ones against their screens. Then there was a bright flash of lightning and; after four stick-in-the-muds, a crack of thunder. I heard Mamma's voice along with the menfolks' and it sounded worried. "Is all the livestock under cover?"

Papa said everything except the chickens and they'd streak for cover as soon as it began to storm. "What do you think it is, Robert?" Mamma asked.

"I dunno," Papa said, "but I sure as hell don't like the sound o' that rumble."

They stayed outside for quite a while. I picked up my albatross and carried it with me to the east window. Papa and Mamma and Jim were all staring at something to the west. I moved to the west window. The sun had disappeared behind a cloud that was almost overhead now. Black and white broomstraws hanging from it hid Comanche, hid everything. Jagged lightning from the cloud would sting the prairie and then the thunder cannonade and roll and crackle.

Mamma came to the door. "We're going to the root cellar—just to be on the safe side," she said. I started toward her and then there was a crash—like a rock dropping on the roof from a cliff a mile high.

I dropped the flatiron and blood gushed from my mouth. I stood staring at it stupidly, thinking Mamma was right, it didn't hurt at all, and then I heard her say, heard Mamma who never in her whole life swore, say, "My God! Oh, my God!"

There was another crash, louder than the first, and then another, and then—for a long moment—that was all. Except the room turned dark as if it was night and the wick in the lamp was as low as it would go and still burn. Papa and Jim came inside, and we all stood looking at each other without saying a word. Shep crawled under the stove. Mamma stared at my bloody mouth but did not seem to see me at all.

I picked up my tooth, put it in my pocket and stuck my tongue in the hole it had left. I tried to tell Papa but he was listening to the train or whatever it was that kept coming and was almost on us. It sounded like the express that you couldn't even flag for life or death when it went through Acton. You had to stand far back on the platform when it passed, Papa had told me, so that it would not suck you under the wheels. I went to Mamma and touched her. She looked down and saw me at last and started to wipe my mouth with her apron when all of a sudden the storm struck in earnest—not a few random hailstones but whole volleys of them, hundreds and thousands of them, hammering, pounding the thin boards of the frail steamboat roof.

Papa shouted something at Mamma but she could not hear. Nobody could hear anything but the hail. I went to the door and looked out. White balls as big as hens' eggs, some as big as baseballs, were bouncing off the roof of the stoop and piling up around the shack. Lightning stabbed the crest of the rise only a couple hundred yards from us, but the explosion of thunder was lost in the barrage of falling ice.

I felt somebody's hand on my shoulder. I looked up. It was Jim. He was trying to shout something at me. He repeated it. I could not hear him, but his lips were saying, "Don't be scared." I looked past him. You could see daylight through the cracks in the roof where the hail had already ripped off the protective tarpaper and was now knocking the knots out of the pine planks onto the floor.

The vents of the kitchen range were belching steam like a dragon. Hailstones had come right down the stovepipe and were melting. Mamma was staring at the stove as if it was hellfire. She was wringing her hands and her lips quivered. Papa put his hand on her arm, but she flinched and drew it away.

Then for a short while the bombardment increased and the whole earth shook. Shep came out from under the stove, his tail between his legs, and howled but I couldn't hear him. We stood still and held our breath. Water poured through the cracks in the roof, but nobody did anything about it. It was as if we were waiting for the ugly dollhouse we lived in to be crushed, as it surely had to be.

And then, almost as suddenly as it had begun, it was over. The devil cloud roared on to the east and let us have the sun again.

We all went out onto the stoop to view the devastation. The prairie was glistening white and steaming in the ravishing sunlight under a four-inch blanket of ice. The garden lay dead beneath it. There was no sign of the wheat, the oats, or the alfalfa.

"I never seen nothin' like it, Mr. Eunson," Jim said.

Papa shook his head. "Well, I'll be goddamned," he muttered.

"No. Not you," Mamma said quietly. "Me."

We all turned and looked at her. "It's a judgment," she said. "God's judgment."

"What you talking about, Jessie?" Papa asked.

She simply stared at him for a long while. It seemed as if she wanted to say something else, but it stuck, and she could not get it out. She turned and walked back into the house. Papa followed her. I could hear his voice but not hers, so I don't know whether she ever answered his question or not.

Jim and I looked out across the field again. Everything else was gone, but we sure had ice from hell to breakfast! It seemed a crying shame to waste it, Jim said. "If we had us a ice-cream freezer, we could freeze us some ice cream for your birthday," he said.

"We got us one," I said. "We brought it with us from Wisconsin."

"Well, what are we waiting for?" Jim said. "Let's shake a leg."

Genevieve and Earl did not get home until two in the morning. The hail had melted by then, so she did not know what had happened until she awoke and looked out the window.

By the time I got up and went down to the coop to open the trap door and let the chickens into the run—we had to close and latch it every night; otherwise a weasel or a coyote might get in—I saw Papa and Genevieve strolling in the field where the wheat had been. As soon as I fed the chickens, I loped off to join them, but Mamma saw me and called after me. I was to help her set the breakfast table, she said.

That didn't make much sense to me. She had never asked me to set the breakfast table before. I was trying to think up some excuse not to do it when Jim, who was toting the warm, fresh milk to the root cellar, said if he was me he wouldn't give my folks any grief today.

"Okay, but it's sure some fine birthday," I said, and turned toward the shack, which looked like a carelessly iced chocolate cake. The sides were still black, but the steamboat roof was a blotch of mangled tarpaper with naked white pine showing through.

Mamma's eyes were red. She said she was afraid she was in for another sick headache; it was because of that terrible racket yesterday. She could still hear it pounding inside her head. As soon as breakfast was over she was going to pull down the shades and go to bed.

Presently Papa, Genevieve, and Jim came in, and we all sat down to breakfast. Nobody was very hungry; nobody said anything about me being seven years old today. It seemed as if everybody was very polite and unnatural—not that we were naturally impolite people, but we usually said what first popped into our heads. This morning even I did not do that. I was doggoned if I was going to be the first one to mention my birthday. It was up to somebody else to do that.

Papa coughed and finally announced that Genevieve was going to leave us. She had spent part of yesterday looking for a job and was going to clerk at Hart-Albin's department store. She had even found a nice family to board and room with. Their name was Smith, and Mr. Smith was steam engineer at the Northern Hotel. They had a daughter Genevieve's age, named Ethel. Ethel played the piano too, so the girls were sure to become great friends.

Mamma listened without any expression at all. She was fighting back the sick headache, I guess. Finally she said, "Genevieve, this will always be your home. I want you to know that."

Genevieve said she knew it, but it was time she went to work, especially now that we'd been hailed out. If things got tough with us, she could help out with her wages. She could probably save a little; she was going to earn $12.50 a week and only had to pay $5 out of that for board and room.

"You're to keep your own money," Papa said gruffly. "We'll get along."

Then they changed the subject, and Genevieve told us about the roundup, but she was careful not to mention the stallions with golden hooves because that was what had started all the fuss, and about supper—only they called it dinner—last night at the Northern, and how afterward Earl had taken her to a moving-picture show about someone named Enoch Arden which lasted for about thirty-five minutes and she got the sniffles when the hero came back after being gone all those years and given up for dead and found his wife married to his best friend, and he had just gone away without letting anybody know he was alive.

Mamma finally interrupted this fascinating account. "When are you leaving us?" she asked, making it sound as if Genevieve was somehow deserting us when we needed her most.

"Tomorrow," Genevieve said. "They want me to start work day after tomorrow."

"Well, if you think it's the right thing for you," Mamma said, "Papa and I won't stand in the way."

"It's not exactly a career as a grand-opera singer," Genevieve snapped, for some reason, "but I'd take a job slinging hash to . . ."

"*Genevieve!*" Papa said. "That's enough."

In the stiff silence that followed this sharp reproof, I began to cloud up. "Don't cry. We'll see Genevieve real often," Papa said. "Whenever we go to Billings. And holidays she'll still come and spend with us."

"It's not that," I wailed. "It seems to me that somebody might remember a person's birthday."

Everybody was sorry. It was merely that in the excitement of the hail yesterday, and now with Genevieve springing this news about going to Billings to live, well, my birthday had got lost in the shuffle. But not really. Mamma had been knitting me a sweater, Papa had given Genevieve three dollars to buy me a new pair of boots, Jim had commissioned her to bring me a box of chocolate creams, and Genevieve herself had found me a BB gun.

"He's only seven years old," Mamma said. "He might—why, he could put his eye out with a thing like that!"

"You said I could get him one, didn't you, Papa?" Genevieve said, and I thought, well, here goes, here we go round the mulberry bush, but I grabbed the BB gun and ran outside with it before anybody could take it away from me. Jim followed and showed me how to feed the BB's into it and cocked it for me—the cocking lever was still too stiff for me to work.

I looked around for something to shoot at and the first thing I saw was a sparrow sitting on the clothesline thirty feet away. I set the stock against my right shoulder, found the sparrow in the sight, and pulled the trigger. The gun popped harmlessly, and the sparrow dropped off the clothesline—dead. I gasped and looked at the terrible thing in my hand. It had not even occurred to me that I might hit the bird!

"Hot damn!" Jim said. "You killed it! I'm going to git you a sharpshooter's medal next time I go to town."

I dropped the BB gun and ran to the privy where I always went, if I had time, when I was going to be sick.

At noon we had the ice cream. It was still frozen, packed in hail and salt in the freezer in the root cellar. Genevieve had made my favorite dessert—a spongecake cut into squares, plastered on all six surfaces with powdered sugar, barely moistened in thick, rich cream, and then dipped in crushed walnuts. I tried to eat. I'd put something in my mouth and swallow, and then I would see that sparrow sitting there, chirping at me on the clothesline, and then see it lying dead on the ground.

It was the worst birthday I ever had.

"I'D BE A MILLIONAIRE TODAY IF I HADN'T BEEN SUCH A DAMN FOOL."

Thirteen

The hailstorm was tough luck, everybody agreed, but not the sort of thing to panic anybody except the rankest tenderfoot. The killing barrage of hail had cut a half-mile, west-to-east swath across the top of the rim. It had only sideswiped the Gullards to the south of us and the Iveses to the northeast. Too bad the Eunsons took the brunt of it, but there probably wouldn't be another ripsnorter like that for ten years, maybe never.

And, Mamma said, making the best of it, we were lucky in a way. We had only forty acres to lose this year. *Next* year we would plant that to hay and at least half the section to winter wheat and, as the fellow said, lightning never strikes twice in the same place, so we'd be safe when the big chips were down.

I don't think Papa bought that Pollyanna line completely, but he was committed by now, so he merely grunted and said, "Mmmm, yeah. Well, that's one way of lookin' at it." He and Uncle Charlie were partners on the section 33 venture. Uncle Charlie had invested his cash in the land, and Papa had taken delivery on the machinery to farm it— the tractor, seeder, and McCormick binder, the John Deere plow, the bunch rake, the mower and baler. He had been counting for seed this fall on the wheat from the twenty-five acres that had been hailed out, but that was small potatoes in the big bucket anyhow, he said. He was in deep now, so what the hell?

He would have to get in deeper, with a loan at the bank, to see us through till next fall. That was one thing he had been hoping to avoid, but things like bank loans—and death and taxes—well, "You better learn to swallow the bitter with the sweet," he would say. "Just throw back your shoulders and dare 'em to get you down."

He was a sentimental, loving man, easily moved to tears, and I suspect he said things like that principally as stern advice to himself to measure up to his own ideal of what a man should be. He had already taken more than enough blows to fell an ordinary mortal. When he was twelve years old his Scottish immigrant father and mother had died, leaving him to find homes for his six younger brothers and sisters. He had lost three infant children by his first marriage, and then my mother. And yet, here he was, fifty-five years old now, starting life all over again as a dryland farmer on the beautiful but pitiless plains of Montana. Tell him there was going to be a party ten miles off and he'd go and be the life of it, dancing off five pounds before Mamma could finally persuade him to go home.

His past must have told him Beware of the Future, but Papa believed that *this—now—today* was all the future there was. "You better grab onto it hard and throw it before it throws you," was his motto.

So, grabbing hold of today and doing what had to be done with it, the first order of business was to prepare the shack for another fall and winter. We were not likely to have two open winters in succession, so we'd better be prepared for the worst. Mamma had never liked the idea of a steamboat roof, white or black. It reminded her of a section hand's shanty. Now, with half the tarpaper ripped off anyhow and the other half riddled with holes, here was the excuse and opportunity to put on a new roof, one that had shingles and pointed toward heaven the way a decent, God-fearing roof should.

Chris Gullard warned against shingling a rim dwelling—the wind she blowed pretty goot sometimes, he said with customary Scandinavian understatement. She could creep in under the shingles, rip them off and scatter them to hell and gone. In fact, don't leave much space under the overhang. Why? Well, first off, he said, it was a waste of money, just for show, and then if you leave the wind a chance to get her fingers in under the roof she might take a little shack like ours, lift it off its foundations, and tumble it across the prairie like a Russian thistle.

Okay, old Chris said, to tack on a gable roof if it would keep the old lady quiet (a condition much to be desired of all females, it would seem), but you take a house like ourn, twelve feet wide, you shouldn't raise the ridgepole more than three, four feet above the eaves or you could find yourself right up that well-known crick with no paddle.

Which, of course, did not create much of an angle to point toward heaven or anywhere else. If the old lady wanted something to point, Chris went on to advise, better we should stick on a pair of lightning rods. Not that they were much protection when the lightning got to popping, but no need to tell the old lady that and get her roiled up. Besides, lightning rods were kind of pretty and gave a house some class.

And so Papa and Jim ripped off the old roof and hammered on a new one, and while they were at it they covered the tarpaper on the outside walls with pine siding. They did not paint it—that was left to Mamma and me—because it was late August and the winter wheat would have to be put in by early October. You couldn't count on the weather after that.

Papa drove the tractor with the four-furrow gang plow behind it from sunup to sundown, while Jim and the team of horses worked behind him with disc and peg-toothed harrow. Mamma had figured that if the tractor traveled four miles per hour and its four plowshares turned a strip fifty-six inches wide Papa could plow the three hundred and twenty acres in fourteen or fifteen days. It was closer to twenty-five by the time he finished.

The tractor broke down twice. It rained for two days, and then you had to let the sod dry out for at least two more before it would slice and turn over without sticking to the plowshares. Far oftener than he had anticipated, Papa had to remove the shares from the moldboards and sharpen them. When a horse-drawn, hand-held plow hit a patch of rocks it would bounce aside, but the gang plow was unwieldy and the tractor powerful. Half the time the driver would not know he was ripping through loose rock or shale until he looked back, and then it was too late to save the plowshares.

Every farmer was his own blacksmith, but during the plowing season incidental jobs like sharpening plowshares were left until the evening chores were done. In September the days were growing shorter. Papa would start the fire in the forge, and while he waited for it to heat up, he would sit down, light his pipe, and puff on it for a minute or two. Sometimes he would get a squinty, far-off look in his eyes. This usually meant he felt like spinning a yarn.

I would sit on the ground and lean my head back on Shep. Jim would be there too—he could help later by holding the white-hot plowshare with the tongs—but sometimes he'd be so dead beat he couldn't keep awake. Papa said that was because Jim was Southern, and a Southerner's blood was thinner than ours on account of the climate down there, and the fact that they'd had slaves to do their work for them until not long ago. Jim meant well; he couldn't help it if he tuckered out faster than we did.

Papa's yarns were not the conventional ones a father tells his son. They were far better, because they were not about princes or magicians or some dumb kid who climbed a beanstalk, but about Papa himself, and they were true. Well, almost true.

There was, for instance, the story of the finale to his logging days. After having been Al Rounds's faithful logging-camp foreman for years and years, Mr. Rounds had offered him three hundred acres of the land they had logged over during the final winter. Papa turned it down cold. It was swampy and covered with stumps. "What the hell good is it?" he had said, but there were no hard feelings. Al Rounds meant well. How unintentionally well even Al Rounds did not know, because that land presently turned out to be part of Oshkosh, Wisconsin. "I'd be a millionaire today if I hadn't been such a damn fool," Papa would say. "And our address would have been Easy Street instead of Acton, Montana."

To prove his lifelong friendship for Al Rounds, when I came along he named me for Al Rounds's son, Dale.

And then there was the story of the two prisoners who escaped from the Clark County Jail.

It seems that these two were not your run-of-the-mill drunks or disturbers of the peace (which was a euphemism for wife-beaters) that the jail usually, and briefly, accommodated. These were horse thieves, and that was much worse. Papa had held them for two weeks while the law took its ponderous time to arraign them. But horse thieves or not, they were members of the human race, so Papa passed the time of day with them when he went back into the tank mornings and evenings. He'd say hello and how were they and was there anything they needed, like soda pop or writing paper in case they wanted to write to their wives or mothers? And on the evening of May 10, 1910 (this part of the story I remembered myself), he had led them, along with three other prisoners, out of the jail so that they could join Mamma and me and our friends on the courthouse lawn for the spectacle of the century. One day, Papa said, they would be able to tell their grandchildren that they had got a look at Halley's comet, courtesy of Sheriff Bob Eunson.

Well, the horse thieves got to know him and, inevitably, to like him. When they escaped—I suspect it was not very difficult to break out of that old jail—they left him a handwritten note which read, "We hate like the devil to do this to you, Sheriff." So far as I know, that was the only time in history that an escapee ever left a note of apology to his jailer.

Nothing was heard of them for two days. Then Papa got a telephone call from his peer, the sheriff of Eau Claire County. He had picked up a couple suspicious characters who vaguely met the description of Bob Eunson's escaped prisoners. He doubted these were the ones—they looked too honest for horse thieves—but he was holding them for a few hours and maybe Papa had better come over and take a look at them.

Papa boarded the next train for Eau Claire. He walked into the cell where the men were being held. They looked at him, grinned, and put out their hands. "Hiya, Bob," they said. "It's good to see you." Papa shook hands with them, then snapped on the handcuffs and took them back to Neillsville. They promised him they would not try to escape again, and they kept their word.

"They seemed like real nice fellas," Papa would say to end the account. Then he'd tamp out his pipe. "They probably just got mixed up with bad company," he'd say, and get to his feet and light the lantern.

"Wake up, Jim. We got a night's work ahead of us."

"I NEED A SCHOOL LIKE I NEED SMALLPOX!"

Fourteen

Mamma was a mover and a shaker and therefore always at her best when she had some project. With the house painted—and you would hardly know the old shack with its new low-gable roof all fancied up by lightning rods, its coat of white paint and green trim—she could turn to thoughts of a schoolhouse.

Here was I, seven years old, ready for the third grade. She could go on teaching me, of course, and did for a while every day, but she did not know the curriculum of Montana schools. When we went to Billings to live—which we would, she announced one day much to Papa's surprise, as soon as we got rich off the wheat—she wanted me ready to take my rightful place at the head of the class in the city school system and not have to waste time making up courses I had missed.

Her petition for a school had paid off. Miraculously, forty-five dollars a month had been apportioned to our district for a teacher's salary. But there was no plan to build a schoolhouse for at least a year, and what good was a teacher without a place for her to teach in?

Again Mamma got on her horse—or rather, my horse—and made the rounds. If the weather stayed mild after everybody's winter crops were in, she had the most wonderful suggestion: why not have a neighborhood schoolhouse-raising bee? It would be a way for us all to get to know each other, a Lark, a Golden Opportunity to Put Our Shoulders to the Wheel and Push Together, and that's what neighbors were for, now wasn't it?

Again she met resistance from almost everyone except the Gullards, What this Lark, this Golden Opportunity really amounted to looked like the devil of a lot of backbreaking labor. And when you came right down to it, what for? For just two kids: Selma Gullard and me. The Torpen children wouldn't be around long enough to make it worthwhile, because the Torpens were figuring on selling out to Al Reynolds.

That, Mamma said reprovingly, was shortsighted. Not only did she hope all would soon be Blessed with Little Ones who could take advantage of a free American education, but suppose you looked at it from a completely practical and selfish point of view: a school increased the value of all property in the district. Land, she said with the authority and conviction of a carnival pitchman, automatically increased at least five dollars an acre the very day the school bell began to ring.

And speaking of school bells, she had put herself and Mr. Eunson down to furnish that item—"besides our share of the lumber." The homesteaders had not heard the ringing of a school bell since they had moved up on the rim. I suspect it was the prospect of hearing that sound once more that did the trick.

The weather stayed mild. In late October we had the raising bee. It took three days, and the neighbors—male and female—all put their shoulders to the wheel and pushed together! At five o'clock of the third day they hung the bell to the bell-post outside the entrance, taking care not to let the clapper strike it accidentally. The first *dingdong* should not be an accident; it should have some significance.

Then everybody went home. The men did the evening chores and put on their Sunday-go-to-meeting clothes. The ladies prepared box lunches, squeezed into their corsets and corset covers, stepped into their dancing togs, and primped their hair.

Almost everybody was back by eight. They tethered their horses, put a stop to several dogfights (in one of which Shep proved a lively contender, though a loser), then tossed mackinaws and sheepskin-lined coats—the temperature was dropping and it felt like snow—in a corner of the little anteroom off the classroom. Wall pegs, where I hung my caps and coats and leggings for the next four years, would come later. So would the big drum-stove, which had been ordered but had not yet arrived.

When we walked in that night, the little schoolroom was, Papa remarked much to Mamma's embarrassment, as cold as a well-digger's butt.

That did not last long. The cold wouldn't stand a Chinaman's chance once the neighbors started to dance.

The scandal of the fox trot and the Castle Walk were not yet even on the horizon. There was the waltz for the romantically inclined young folks and the schottische for the oldsters who could remember the steps and figures, but all that was fancy frills and frippery to be briefly tolerated. The real business of the evening was the square dance and the Virginia reel.

We had a fiddler from up Broadview way, and Papa himself could call the dances, while he danced, better than anybody who could be hired. He and Mamma were both wonderful dancers. Mamma might stop to get her breath and wipe her brow with her handkerchief, but Papa would dance till the cows came home. When he and his partner were supposed to await their turn to "swing your partner and balance on the corner," Papa kept his feet from getting cold by doing a jig.

At midnight we all went outside. It was beginning to snow. Since Mamma was the prime mover in the enterprise, she was awarded the privilege of ringing the bell for the first time. Somebody doused it with a glass of punch (which that devil Peterson had spiked), and then Mamma grabbed the bell rope and pulled, and the bell let go with its first peal. Horses whinnied and dogs barked, and everybody laughed and cried. The men pounded each other on the back and hugged the ladies. Somebody proposed a toast to Mrs. Eunson.

Mamma accepted it as her due. "I only did what needed to be done," she said in a transparent attempt at modesty. "You men folks did all the work."

"Yay, Jessie," Peterson laughed, "but you put the harness on us. Hell and damnation, I need a school like I need smallpox!" Peterson's face was flushed. The punch was not strong enough for him, and he had disappeared several times to go outside for a nip.

"You need what is *right,*" Mamma said. She was out to reform and save Peterson if it was not too late. What he needed (after his tragic experience with that creature who had driven him to drink—the creature Mamma had made right up out of whole cloth but who was now as real to her as that notorious Cattle Kate who had done God knows what down in Wyoming) was a good woman, she had told Papa. Possibly the new schoolteacher arriving tomorrow would be a candidate.

Then the box lunches were auctioned off—the receipts to help pay for the stove if it ever showed up. Jim Harper splurged and went up to sixty-five cents for the box with a blue ribbon. Mamma, it seemed, had slipped him the word that it belonged to Kate Moody, and she had noticed that Jim had been staring at Kate all evening. Kate was fifteen, which was just about right for Jim, who had never been sweet on a girl before.

But to Papa, eating and talking were a waste of time when he might be dancing. Besides, as soon as the dancers stopped moving, the cold began to creep back into the room. "We're paying this damn fiddler good money," he finally said. "Choose your partners for the Virginia reel."

Mamma and Papa woke me at sunup—which was about 6:15. I had finally gone to sleep, curled up with Shep on the stack of outer garments in the anteroom. When we went outside to get in the buggy, there were four inches of snow on the ground. It was still snowing hard and beginning to blow.

At home, Mamma got breakfast while Jim and Papa did the chores. After we had eaten they took the wagon box off the wagon and bolted on the runners and Mamma drove alone to Acton to meet the train, which was bringing the new teacher. (She would live with us temporarily. Papa and Mamma would give her their bedroom until she could find a more suitable place to board.)

While Mamma was gone, Papa and Jim went to work at what they had been putting off while they helped build a schoolhouse: nailing on the new storm windows and then chinking them for the winter. I gave up and went to bed after I let Shep sneak in.

I woke after a little while to see Papa standing beside me. He shook his head when he saw Shep there on the floor under the cot, growling. He was protecting me from my own father!

"Some farm dog," Papa muttered. "He's just no damn good!"

"He's good for me," I said, reaching down and touching his cold nose. "See, he's stopped growling."

"Sure," Papa said, "but we need us a real shepherd dog, now that we're getting more cattle and horses."

"I know you don't want to spend money on another dog," I said, fully awake at the threat to Shep, "but maybe I could win one for you."

"How come?" Papa sat down on the cot beside me.

"Well, it says in the *Saturday Evening Post* how they got white collies, real champeens, that you can win if you sell enough subscriptions."

Papa grinned. "Who'd you sell subscriptions to?"

"Well," I said, "there's Peterson . . ."

"If you catch him when he's well oiled," Papa interrupted. "And who else?"

"Why, our neighbors," I said. "I'll bet a lot of them would subscribe."

"About three—if you were lucky," Papa said. He leaned over and kissed me on the cheek. He hadn't shaved since yesterday, and his beard was rough.

"It was just an idea," I said.

"Go back to sleep. I'll come in and get Shep out of here when I see your mamma coming."

Papa had recently added a woodshed at the side of the house. That was where Shep was supposed to sleep. The cold could not penetrate a dog's heavy winter coat, at least that was what Mamma claimed. But she also said that she could not abide a doggy odor in the house; she had such sensitive olfactory nerves that she could tell when Shep had been inside for as long as twenty-four hours afterward. That, I had discovered, was not 100 percent true. Her olfactory nerves would tell her for twenty-four hours if she had actually *seen* Shep inside. Otherwise, they kept the secret.

"Thanks, Papa," I said.

"AND JUST WHAT
MIGHT COW CHIPS BE?"

Fifteen

The new teacher's name was not Miss Emily Freeman, but I will call her that. Fortunately I cannot remember her real name. If she is still alive, she would probably be mad as hops to read what Mamma and Papa really thought about her. Quite simply, neither of them liked her a little bit. She was almost, but not quite, as old as Mamma and had never married. ("That's nothing against a woman," I heard Mamma say to Papa, very pleasantly, but with a significant lift of an eyebrow—I was not supposed to be old enough to interpret the lifting of an eyebrow—"but I'll venture to say it's not for want of trying.")

Miss Freeman was a gentlewoman—and she was the first

to call your attention to that in case you hadn't noticed—who had been born in Kansas. That was a fatal error in judgment, from the way Papa talked. If you had the misfortune to be born there when you had a choice of forty-seven other states, the least you could do was make your getaway the first chance you got and never call attention to the stigma. I don't know why Papa felt that way about Kansas, but it made sense to me. Hadn't Dorothy taken the first cyclone out? ("Sensible girl!" would have been Papa's reaction had he ever read *The Wizard of Oz.*)

But Miss Freeman had stayed on there until she was thirty, and she talked about it incessantly. Salina, Kansas, to hear her tell it, was the fountainhead of Western culture and manners, and when it came to society, *well!* New York's four hundred were vulgar, new-rich pretenders.

Miss Freeman let us know from the moment she walked in that she was used to better things. "Is *this* where I am to lay my weary bones?" she asked when Mamma showed her the bedroom she and Papa were relinquishing to her.

"Unless you'd rather lay them in the bunkhouse," Mamma said.

"But I thought you told me you had a hired man."

"So I did," Mamma said, very flat.

Miss Freeman sputtered, turned red, and shut the bedroom door.

School started next day, not in the new schoolhouse, because the stove still hadn't arrived, but in Julia Adams's shack to the west of us. Miss Adams had red hair and had once been a music teacher, we had heard. What brought her to a homestead alone in Acton we never knew. If a person did not volunteer such information, it was impolite to ask.

She had to live there for one more six-month session

before she could prove up on her homestead, but it was October and she left for Billings before there was much chance of a blizzard. We were welcome to her castle, such as it was, she had said. At least it had a stove in it, if somebody would chop and haul wood to stuff it with.

Papa said guess who's elected? He went down early and started the fire the first day so the chill would be off when Miss Freeman and us kids got there. Miss Freeman had let us know the night before that starting a wood fire was in the nature of a mystery to a gentlewoman like herself.

"What did your folks use for fuel?" Mamma smiled when she asked. "Cow chips?"

"And just what might cow chips be?" Miss Freeman asked, falling right into Mamma's trap.

"Dried cow manure," Mamma said, "and nothing to be ashamed of when you can't afford wood."

"That's not what I meant," Miss Freeman snapped.

"How was I to know?" Mamma said.

"She's not as helpless as she puts on," I heard Mamma whisper that night after she and Papa went to bed—on the floor. "She just wants a man—any old man, so she can bat her eyelashes and simper and show him how smart he is. Don't you let her get away with it, Robert!"

"You know what," Papa whispered. "I think you're jealous of Miss Freeman."

"*Her?*" Mamma snorted.

"Yes, she's too high-toned for you," Papa said, joshing her.

"Oh, fuf!" Mamma said, laughing. "If that's what you think's high-toned!"

"What was all that talk about you going to introduce the

new schoolmarm to Peterson?" Papa asked, knowing the answer but wanting to hear Mamma say it.

"I wouldn't wish that one on Pancho Villa," Mamma obliged him with.

I giggled at that. Mamma said, "Dale, you're supposed to be asleep."

"I am," I said. "I must have been laughing in my sleep."

"You're not to repeat one word of what you heard us say. Not to a soul! Promise?"

"Promise," I repeated. "But are we going to have her all year?"

"We'll see," Mamma said. And I knew right then that Miss Freeman's days were numbered.

Yet Mamma had a problem, especially serious to her, since it was not in her nature to say "I made a mistake." She had fought for and promoted the school. Since she had gone that far, the neighbors were more than willing to lay the burden of selecting a teacher on her shoulders. It was she who had gone to Billings, talked to the superintendent of schools of Yellowstone County, and okayed the credentials and application of one Miss Emily Freeman.

How then could she go to the parents and neighbors and tell them Miss Freeman was not the right teacher? "Why isn't she?" they would have a right to ask. "Did you buy a pig in a poke?"

I do not know whether Miss Freeman was a good teacher or not. I was only seven years old. I did not like her, but that could have been a reflection of how Mamma and Papa felt about her. In the years that followed, I had many teachers and my liking or disliking them had very little to do with their ability to pry open my mind to the world's wisdom.

A boy's liking or disliking a teacher, I realize thinking back, is a matter of animal chemistry—a subtle odor of body, breath, and hair as she leans over your desk to examine your paper, the tone of voice as she says "Good morning, class," the look on her face while she waits as you flounder for the answer to a question, a look that can make you feel like an imbecile or that with a little more application you will stand at the head of the class. That's why you like or dislike a teacher.

I do know that the others in school that last week in October and the first in November shared my dislike. (Had I brought it to them from home, I wonder?) There were six of us on the good days—the four Torpen kids, who lived on a claim southwest of us, two girls and two boys, all older than me, ranging from fourth to eighth grade; and Selma Gullard, who was twelve and in the sixth grade. We made fun of Miss Freeman's mannerisms. "Let's all . . . breeeeeathe!" she would cry happily first thing in the morning after she called us to order.

Breathing was something Selma and I at least had never paid much attention to. We had been doing it all our lives. We breathed fast when we were tired or scared, and slow when we were going to sleep. Well, it seems we had been doing it wrong. Miss Freeman would stand very straight before us, heels together, toes at a 90-degree angle, chest thrown out until you'd think her camisole would pop, and then say, "Here we go, my hearties! Now . . . *breathe* . . . Innnn. . . Hold, that's the important thing, hold, hold a little little longer now . . . Ouuuuut . . . Hold, hold till you think you can't stand it and then hold a little little longer. . . . Innnnnn. . . hooooooooold. . . Ouuuuuuut."

Mamma happened to be visiting school one day when she did that.

Meanwhile, as the two weeks passed, Miss Freeman would borrow Fly to tour the neighborhood, looking for more suitable quarters. "Take your time," Mamma told her. "Don't move and then find you've got to move again."

And then one night Earl Hickson came by and stayed for supper. As luck would have it, he got to talking about snakes—rattlesnakes. Earl said he had rattlesnakes to thank for his homestead.

"Rattlesnakes?" Miss freeman said, sucking in her breath. "Are there rattlers up here?"

"Scads of 'em, ma''am," Earl said. "You got to watch where you step around these parts." Anyhow, it seemed that a man named Loren Lord had originally filed a couple years ago on what was now Earl's land. He was a real authentic tenderfoot, and when the rattlers crawled out of hibernation the spring of 1910 and commenced to rattle, he hotfooted it to Billings and relinquished his claim. Earl, who had been a cowboy for Al Reynolds, had had his eye on that piece of land for quite some time, so he filed on it.

"Are there snakes around now?" Miss Freeman asked. She turned quite pale.

"I guess they've got to be around somewhere," Earl said, "but they're sluggish and harmless once it turns cold."

Miss Freeman wanted to know where they went in winter.

"Down prairie-dog holes, under rocks, any old place for protection," Earl told her.

"And under houses," Mamma said. "Julia Adams told me about one that slithered under her shack last summer before she could whack its head off with her hoe."

"Something's the matter with Miss Freeman," Jim said. "Danged if she don't look like she's fixin' to faint."

"Just breathe innnnnnn . . ." said Mamma, looking at her with sympathy. "Hooooooooold . . . and then breathe Ouuuuuuuuttt."

Miss Freeman gave notice and finished out the week. She simply could not find a suitable place for a gentlewoman to board.

"WHEN YOUR TIME COMES, YOU BETTER BE PACKED AND READY."

Sixteen

"Now," Mamma said. "I—that is, we—shall do what we should have done right at the start."

That was to nominate Edna Moody for country schoolteacher. Edna would not require coddling or acclimatizing. She had already lived on the Moody homestead for two years. She was a hard worker, dependable, practical and modest and, as Papa said, she didn't have marbles where her brains ought to be. Furthermore, you couldn't scare her with the mere mention of rattlers. By the time she was seventeen she had killed four of them herself, three with a hoe and one with a blacksnake whip. She never turned a hair. Her glasses merely steamed up a little.

Edna was young and had not attended normal school, but in an emergency such as ours these details could be waived so long as she had a high-school diploma. Edna had one. And she had another thing going for her: her sister, Kate. Kate, who had not yet finished high school, could substitute in case Edna took sick.

The big drum-stove finally arrived and was installed—and never worked very well. The drum around it was advertised as preventing fire or burns if you brushed against it, while letting heat radiate gently from the larger surface. But on cold days the radiation was far too gentle. What we needed to blast up the temperature after it had dropped to zero or below during the night was an old-fashioned pot-bellied stove that had a good, roaring draft and would glow red hot in a matter of twenty minutes or so.

But we were stuck with the fancy drum-stove and as a result the coat-and-cap pegs in the anteroom were empty on the coldest days of winter. We sat at our desks with overshoes, leggings, coats, caps, and mittens on. Holding a pencil in the hand was out of the question. But that was one of the nice things about having Miss Moody. She understood and did not expect the impossible. She was *really* a gentlewoman.

I have used the term "we" loosely. The Torpens were strictly sunshine scholars. They would be kept home on rainy days and even when the mercury in the thermometer fell below 20 degrees—20 degrees above zero, that is. This would not faze Selma Gullard and me—or rather, our parents would not let it. I would usually wait until I saw Selma riding her horse, or walking, across Julia Adams's homestead; then Shep and I would hurry to meet her, and the three of us would go the rest of the way together.

When it was snowing, Mamma would look out the window around twenty minutes past eight and shake her head. "I guess Selma isn't going to make it today," she would say. "You'd better go on alone."

"Do I have to?"

"Do you want to grow up to be an ignoramus?"

On such days "we" were Shep and me. Miss Moody would even let Shep come into the schoolroom. She would pat him on the noggin and say, "We won't tell anybody if you won't," and Shep would wag his tail as if he understood.

The first time she said that I was not sure it was supposed to be a joke, because Jim had once told me about going to Hagenbeck's Circus, where they had a talking dog in one of the sideshows. It could say "Mamma" as plain as paint, he said, and other words too, but Jim could not understand them because the dog was speaking Polish. The man who owned him was from Poland, and it was there in the old country that he taught the dog to talk. In Poland, he said, everybody could understand the dog, but here in America he had to interpret what the dog said. Once a dog learned a language, it was almost impossible to teach him another, it seemed.

I told Miss Moody that, and she merely smiled. "I'd be inclined to take that with a grain of salt," she said.

"Oh, no," I said. "Jim saw the dog himself. His name was Ignatz. And it said on the banner right outside the tent, 'Ignatz, the dog that talks!' "

Miss Moody turned and looked at Shep, who was staring at the stove. "Shep," she said, "what are you thinking about? What would you say if you could talk?"

"Oh, I know," I said. "He's thinking, how come I don't

warm up when I lie beside this stove? Why isn't this stove hot like our stove?"

"I'll bet he is at that," Miss Moody said. "Now let's forget talking dogs and turn to page 74 of our arithmetic."

We settled down to the routine of winter.

The days were short and the sun so muted you could stare right at it without blinking an eye. It did not climb up over the rim until well after seven, when the milking had already been done by lantern light. Then it hugged the horizon for about nine hours and finally snugged down behind the Absarokas by four-fifteen for the fifteen-hour night. On days before a blizzard, sun dogs kept it company across the southern sky. Sometimes there were two; once in a while four glimmered eerily in rainbow pastels.

Between the two of them, Papa and Mamma could do all the winter chores so Jim went off to Billings and got himself a job washing dishes at the Commercial Hotel. To insure his returning to us in the spring, Mamma suggested that he leave his bearskin and his .22 in the bunkhouse. Jim would not be apt to vamoose without those prize possessions, she said.

Christmas came on Monday that year, and Genevieve was going to come home for three days. On the Thursday preceding the long holiday weekend, Papa went to the rim and cut us a trim little spruce. That night and Friday we decorated it with strings of cranberries and popcorn and apples. Genevieve was to bring the star for the point and the candles and candleholders.

Saturday morning Papa went to meet the train at Acton. Mamma was busy stuffing eggs, frying chicken for the Christmas party at the schoolhouse that evening, and pressing her white satin dress. I might as well make the cake, she decided. Mamma had set herself the task of teaching me to cook. Papa could barely fry an egg, and she said that she dreaded to think what would happen if the two of us were left alone. If she ever had to be away from home, she wanted us to miss her and not just her cooking, she said. (As it turned out, her foresight paid dividends all too soon.)

When Papa came in with Genevieve wearing her new coonskin coat and hat we knew something was wrong. He tried to tell us, but the only word he could get out of his mouth was, "Jim . . . Jim," before he turned and bolted from the house.

"Jim" meant Jim Harper to me, and from the way Papa acted, something awful must have happened to him, but Genevieve set me right. "Uncle Jim is dead," she said and started to cry.

Uncle Jim was two years younger than Papa. He and his wife, Aunt Ella, had lived for many years in Wausau. They used to come to visit us in Neillsville or we would go to Wausau at least three or four times a year. There had been a close bond between the two brothers, who had been orphaned back in 1868, and being so far from Uncle Jim had been one of the reasons Papa was reluctant about coming to Montana. Now he was dead, and Papa would never see him again, wouldn't even be able to go to his funeral.

Aunt Ella had been unable to get in touch with us direct, but she corresponded with Genevieve, so she sent her a telegram in Billings.

Genevieve wiped her eyes and blew her nose. Mamma was a little misty too. "Of course I haven't known your

Uncle Jim nearly as long as you have, Genevieve," she said, "but I was very fond of him, and I think he liked me too."

"I know he did," Genevieve said. "He told me."

"Why, daughter," Mamma said, surprised and delighted, "how nice of you to tell me that."

I have the feeling that if Mamma had not called Genevieve "daughter" at that moment, the two of them might have buried the hatchet. But neither one of them could help rubbing the other the wrong way.

I went outside and led the team down to the barn. I started to go inside, but Papa was making a strangling sound that came right through the door, so I waited. After a little while the noise let up, the door opened, and Papa came out wiping his eyes and his nose on the sleeve of his mackinaw.

"I'm awful sorry, Papa," I said.

"He was a good man," Papa said, and then he looked at me and took my chin in his hand and turned my face first one way, then another. "You know," he said, "you favor Jim the way I remember him as a boy your age. You favor Jim even more than your dad. Then, of course, all us Eunsons look alike."

He unhitched the horses and led them into the barn. I watched him hang up the collars and harnesses, and then he curried old Babe and Sam—automatically, as if his mind was on something else, as of course it was.

This was my first brush with death, the first time I had ever known someone who was now dead, whatever "dead" meant. It gave me a funny feeling. We would go back to Wausau some day and see Aunt Ella, but Uncle Jim would not be there. He'd be in the graveyard.

"Why do good people die?" I asked.

"Good people, bad people, that don't cut no ice," Papa said. "When your time comes, you better be packed and ready to go, because the train don't wait for no man."

"I'm never going to die," I said.

"Good for you," Papa said absently.

He put the blankets over the horses so they would not cool off too fast, and I peeked into the chicken coop to see if there were any eggs that ought to be gathered before they froze and cracked. Then we started off toward the house. I wanted to ask another question that I knew I had no business asking at a time like this. That such a thought could even occur to me would show that I had no respect for Uncle Jim. But maybe, I thought, maybe if I said it so that it sounded as if I just took it for granted that we weren't going, then it wouldn't be so bad.

"Mamma had me make a cake for the party tonight," I said, "but I guess we'll be eating it at home now, huh?"

"Hell, no," Papa said. "There's nothing more I can do for Jim. If he thought I was staying home from a dance on account of his shaking off his mortal coil, he'd say I was one damned hypocrite."

It was in February that Shep began to talk to me. Well, not really talk; he didn't need to do that. I knew what he was thinking, that's all.

The winter had been cruel and bitter. The Arctic blasts swept down out of Great Slave Lake and left icy calling cards at Edmonton and Calgary, Medicine Hat and Moose Jaw, Cut Bank and Great Falls. Then it was sucked into the funnel between the Big Snowies and the Little Belts. Around Judith Gap it blew so hard on some days that a man could not stand upright against it, and if he called for help he'd better be calling with the wind. Otherwise, no one would hear him.

Then it roared out of its temporary confinement and came hell-bent for the rim!

At night the north wind was a banshee—or was that wailing a lonesome timber wolf or a coyote? When it came in on the heels of a snowstorm it slammed the snow through keyholes and the tiniest cracks and crevices. My cot stood under a window, and during the night I could feel snow sifting in across my face.

There was a special technique of getting undressed and into bed on such nights. The routine of taking off your clothes and then slipping the nightgown over the head was reversed. Put on the nightgown, *then* remove your clothes from under it. That way you might avoid starting your teeth to chattering.

Though we had outing flannel sheets and nightgowns—pajamas, like radio, had not yet been invented—the first plunge beneath the half-dozen blankets took the breath away. Then you would have to lie perfectly still in one spot, your legs hiked up under you. Gradually that spot would warm. Then cautiously you put one leg down and finally the other.

Then, the lamp turned out, there was nothing but the wind huffing and puffing at the house. It would shudder and creak, and the taut wires anchoring the stovepipe screeched like the E-string of a country fiddle. Sometimes the wind would pause, as if getting ready for a new and prolonged blast, and in the silence would come the antiphonal melody of a coyote or timber wolf howling out its hunger and loneliness.

But you were snug and warm and asleep at last.

And then it would be morning, and the wind still blew. Even the snow tried to get away from it in long, ten-foot drifts streaking south from any building. But it was time for school once more, and on days like this there was not much to look forward to. A walk or ride through the wind, and then just Miss Moody, Shep, and me.

"DOGS ARE VERY SENSITIVE CREATURES."

Seventeen

Mamma was not well.

She did not tell Papa until the pain got so bad that he could see it on her face. Then she admitted she had been having pains in her side for some little time. She had not mentioned it because she thought it would go away. Plenty of pains came and simply went away if you paid no attention to them. When you lived twenty miles and four hours from a doctor, you did not make a fuss over every little toe ache. A homestead up on the rim was no place for a hypochondriac.

But Papa said this pain in her side did not sound like a mere toe ache to him. He had been planning to go to

Billings next week anyhow to prove up on the homestead, so he would step it up a week and Mamma could go with him.

It had not snowed for a month. The ground was frozen solid, and patches of ice were left over from the January thaw. They would take the buggy; that would be easier on Mamma and not jiggle her so much as the wagon.

By the time they woke me up the livestock was fed, the cow milked, the stalls cleaned. They were ready to leave. It was six-thirty. They would be home in time to do the evening chores, hopefully before dark.

"But if something happens and we're not, you know how to light the lamp," Papa said.

"I've done it a hundred times."

"Yes, but that's when we've been here."

"I'll be careful."

"And about starting the fire again this afternoon," Papa said. "Don't light the paper outside the stove. Put it in, *under* the kindling, and then light it."

"I *know,* Papa."

"And if it warms up today and thaws out the clothes on the line, bring them in when you get home from school," Mamma said.

"I will."

"I put the bridle and surcingle on Fly," Papa said.

"Thanks."

It was the first time I had ever been in the house all alone—well, not quite alone, because as soon as they were out of sight I let Shep in—and I liked it. I didn't have to do anything I didn't want to, like brushing my teeth or going all the way to the privy for Number One. Mamma had left plenty of batter for pancakes for the two of us

"Dogs Are Very Sensitive Creatures." 141

and I even put butter and corn syrup on Shep's. After he ate the first one, he looked up at me and said "Thanks." Not out loud, you understand—silently, but I could hear him.

We started for school in plenty of time, because Papa had warned me about making Fly gallop. She was getting a little heavy around the middle, and galloping wouldn't be good for the colt she was carrying. With the increased dimension of her already round little back, riding her at a trot was a little like riding a barrel through mild rapids, not dangerous but tricky. I would constantly have to go for leather and grab the surcingle to keep from bouncing off—which would be humiliating if anybody chanced to see me.

It was still and cold and the sky was gray. We took our usual trail across the southwest corner of section 29. Fly wanted to run but I held her back, so it was nobody's fault that she slipped on a patch of ice and fell with my right foot under her.

It did not hurt me at all, but I wondered if a fall like that would be bad for the colt. Fly scrambled to her feet and waited patiently while I took a running jump over her rump and landed squarely on her back again.

By the time we got to school my foot felt stiff. When I slid off Fly's back a pain shot up my leg. It was easier to hop on my left leg than to step on the right one while I tied Fly up in the animal shed beside Miss Moody's pony and gave her her oats.

Miss Moody had the fire going but the thermometer inside still read 40 degrees. She took one look at me and knew something was wrong. I guess I was paler than usual. I told her about the fall and how I hoped nothing would happen to Fly's colt, and she said she guessed I'd better take my high-topped shoe off and let her examine my foot.

That was easier said than done. Loosening the two buckles at the top and unlacing it was simple, but when we came to the shoe itself, and I tried to pull that off, I yelped. I didn't want to, but I couldn't help it. Miss Moody tried but that hurt even more. She finally got the scissors out of her desk. I asked her what she was going to do, and she said we were going to have to cut the shoe down the side so we could ease it off.

The high-topped shoes were my birthday present from Papa. I told Miss Moody that she'd better not cut into the leather because Papa would be mad, but she seemed to think he would understand and went right ahead. "I'll take the responsibility," she said.

Finally the shoe came off, and the pressure was released. My foot no longer hurt, but by the time I'd pulled my stocking down it was puffing up like a Fourth of July balloon made in the shape of a foot.

Miss Moody made a clucking sound with her tongue and said she didn't like the looks of it.

"It doesn't hurt now," I said. Nevertheless, she had better take me home, Miss Moody said.

"But what if another pupil comes and you're not here?"

"Selma would be the only other child on a cold day like this and she's got a cold so her father wouldn't let her come," Miss Moody said.

I was pulling my stocking back on when she noticed that Shep was whining. "Dogs are very sensitive creatures," she said. "He somehow knows that you've hurt yourself."

"He knows everything," I said. "Don't you, Shep?"

He lifted his paw to shake hands and suddenly I realized something was bothering him.

"What are you trying to say, Shep?" Miss Moody asked.

"He's just reminding me that nobody's at home today," I said, explaining about Mamma having to go to the doctor. In all the excitement I had forgotten.

"Well, thank you, Shep," Miss Moody said.

That changed everything, of course. There was no sense taking me home to be alone all day, so we pretended it was like any other school day except that Miss Moody piled some firewood beside my desk, draped a horse blanket over it, and I sat with my foot up on that. When I let it hang down it throbbed, but up on the wood pile I did not feel a thing.

Miss Moody took me home in midafternoon. The Moody homestead was to the southwest, not actually up on the rim proper. Going home from our place would mean she had to double back. Her father always wanted her to be home by dark. I told her I was sure I could make it home alone if she would give me a hoist up on Fly, but she said she would not feel right about letting me take off alone. Suppose I was to fall off? How would I get back on? In fact, we'd better lead Fly and both of us ride her horse.

She lifted me up and put me on the apron of the saddle behind her. Then I was glad I hadn't tried to go home alone. The foot throbbed when it hung at the side, so Miss Moody held it up with her right hand.

She put Fly in the barn and gathered the few eggs that had been laid during the day. I told her I was supposed to bring in the clothes if they'd thawed out, but they were still stiff as boards so she left them. Then she came into the house and started the fire. "I think I'd better light the lamp, too," she said. "Standing on one foot, you might knock it over."

It was still daylight and it seemed a waste to burn the kerosene when we didn't need to, but she lit it anyway. "Waste not, want not, until the crop is in," Papa used to say, and laugh. "Then Powder River, let 'er buck!"

"There," Miss Moody said, glancing around the room. "You sure you're not afraid to stay by yourself awhile?"

"I'm not by myself. Shep's here," I said.

"I keep forgetting that," Miss Moody said, looking down at him. "He's quite a remarkable dog, isn't he?"

"He's my friend," I said, "and I can understand what he says to me, too."

"I've noticed that," Miss Moody said, smiling. "But you know something? Let's keep that a secret. Other people might think it was funny."

"Why?"

"Well, it's most unusual. Not many dogs can talk."

"You mean somebody might want to take him and put him in a circus?"

"They might."

Shep and I watched Miss Moody until she was out of sight. Then he said he was hungry, so I fixed us both some bread and milk. After that I sat down on the piano stool and made a few stabs at "When You Wore a Tulip and I Wore a Red Red Rose," without even practicing my scales first. But the keys were icy and my foot ached so it was no fun to break the rules.

I sat down in Papa's big chair, put my foot up on the fender of the pot-bellied stove, and picked up Mamma's new book, *Sister Carrie,* which she had told me I was too young to read yet awhile. The print was too small for a

"Dogs Are Very Sensitive Creatures."

boy of seven, she said, even though I was going on eight. It might strain my eyes.

The next thing I knew I woke up and it was dark outside. I looked at the clock. It said 9:30. Then I heard Molly bawling her head off, and no wonder! It was way past milking time and her bag would be all swollen up. I knew just how she must feel, because my foot was swollen even worse than it had been. I felt like bawling too.

The fire was about to go out so I hopped to the woodshed, brought in some wood, and stuffed it into the stove, then opened the damper to get it started fast.

Only then did I wonder what had happened. Papa had said they would try to be home by dark, but at the outside not later than six. Here it was twenty minutes to ten. I went to the door and listened for the clop-clop of old Sam, but there was no sound except Molly's distress signal and the distant barking of the Gullards' dog, Buster, which we could sometimes hear on a clear night. Then there was another sound, farther off: the howl of a wolf from the edge of the rim to the south. That was probably what had set Buster off. Shep was about to join the chorus but I shut the door because I had begun to shiver.

What had happened? Had Sam got scared of an automobile in Billings and run away? Had they slipped over the cliff going around Holdup Hill?

I shook harder and got down on the floor beside Shep and put my arms around him. Shep was worrying too. He was thinking: What are we going to do if they're dead? I told him it wasn't very polite to consider yourself first. He ought to be worrying about *them*. But I couldn't really blame him because no matter how smart he was, he was still just a dog and at the mercy of some human. Oh, I was his master and he knew how I felt about him, but I suppose he realized I was just a kid at the mercy of *my* folks, who didn't feel the way I did about him.

I, too, was having a personal problem that was not really worthy of me at such a moment. I needed to go to the backhouse and kept putting it off. I told myself that the wolf had to be at least two miles off and even if he started lickety split the minute he heard me open the door he couldn't make it to our place before I got back inside. And even if he did, Shep would protect me. But it wouldn't be fair to ask Shep to do that because Papa said your average dog wouldn't be any better off than a snowball in hell beside a timber wolf, and Shep already bore the scars of a bear. Besides, what if I slipped and fell and broke my other leg?

I used the slop jar. I hoped I could make Mamma understand why.

I sat down again and picked up the old faithful *Wizard of Oz* and started all over again, reading it aloud.

"Dorothy lived in the midst of the great Kansas prairies, with Uncle Henry, who was a farmer, and Aunt Em, who was the farmer's wife. Their house was small, for the lumber to build it had to be carried by wagon many miles. There were four walls, a floor and a roof, which made one room; and this room contained a rusty-looking cooking stove, a cupboard for the dishes, a table, three or four chairs, and the beds.' "

"Just like this room before Papa built on the bedroom," I explained to Shep. "Except we always had a piano."

Then Papa was picking me up in his arms and putting me to bed. It was a minute before I could remember what had happened, because I had gone to sleep, so I told him all about my foot before I even thought to ask about Mamma, who didn't seem to be there.

She wouldn't be home, Papa said, for about three weeks. It was lucky they went to Billings today, or it might have been too late. She had appendicitis and the appendix burst just as they got downtown. Probably the jiggling of the buggy on the hard-frozen road had done it, though he'd tried to drive as carefully as he could. He had hurried her straight to St. Vincent's hospital and they had operated right away—to avoid peritonitis, or blood poisoning—but he couldn't leave her until she came out of the ether and he could rest easy knowing she was going to pull through.

Papa would go to Billings once a week to see her— Genevieve could bring her whatever she needed—and one of the Gullard boys could come over to do the chores for us and spend the nights with me.

"It's lucky Mamma's teaching me to cook," I told him.

"On one leg?"

"Sure. See?" I showed him how I could hop.

He picked me up again and carried me into the bedroom. We would sleep together while Mamma was laid up. He put me down on the bed and then felt of my foot.

"Does it hurt?"

"Only when you press on it right *there*." I showed him where.

"You probably got a fracture. Maybe I better take you down to the doctor next time I go to see Mamma," he said.

"No. It'll be all right."

Papa cut my stilts down and made crutches out of them but they were a nuisance. I could hop faster. I hopped for three weeks—cooking, gathering the eggs, cleaning out the chicken coop, bringing in water from the well and, now that Papa was home, even making it to the backhouse after dark.

By the time Mamma came home three weeks later—paler and thinner and strangely subdued—I was able to walk on the foot again. I could only feel a twinge now and then when my shoe was laced too tight.

Funny . . . Almost sixty years later I still can, on rainy days.

"JIM, BE SURE TO
SHOW FERN YOUR
BEARSKIN."

Eighteen

The hospital and doctor bills had made quite a dent in Papa's pangabook, as he called his wallet. St. Vincent's had charged five dollars a day, plus the cost of the operating room and the anesthetist's fee, and the doctor had had the unmitigated gall to hold Papa up for a hundred dollars for the operation. He had got us mixed up with J. P. Morgan, Papa said, or maybe he thought money grew on trees. Hell, we didn't even have any trees!

However, there'd be no more hospital or doctor bills, Mamma said. Those were things of the past because she had become a Christian Scientist. Or rather, as she put it, she was now "in Science." She did not have the presumption to consider herself a full-fledged Scientist yet; there was much to study, much to learn. The neophyte approached Parnassus a step at a time, but she had taken the first firm step by purchasing the textbook, *Science and Health with Key to the Scriptures*, by Mary Baker Eddy.

Mamma had had the good fortune to share her hospital room with a lady who had broken her leg in a tumble down her stairs. Her name was Mrs. Schultz, and she had been immobilized for weeks within a spider web of ropes and pulleys and weights while the thighbone knit. As everyone knew, the knitting of bones was a painful process, but Mrs. Schultz smiled constantly and never uttered a word of complaint. She even insisted that there was no pain. Pain was mortal error.

Since she was such a pure soul, Mamma had at first wondered how God could permit such an accident to happen to her, but Mrs. Schultz explained that it was malicious animal magnetism, which was a sort of evil emanation from those who were jealous of your perfection. Unless you were on the lookout constantly, MAM, as she abbreviated it, could come between you and God. Besides, the accident had happened quicker than two shakes of a lamb's tail so she had not had the opportunity to call upon Him to prevent it.

Mamma took up Science with a vengeance. Not only did it bring her peace of mind to know that she was God's perfect child—as was I and as was Papa, usually, except when he swore or got a twinge of rheumatism in his shoulder and insisted that neither God nor the devil could help him raise his arm—but it was a very practical religion, as Mamma herself could testify.

If only she had been in Science then she would have

called upon God to ease the pain and suppress the inflammation of the appendix, and *He* would have responded. She might have needed the assistance of the practitioner—that was what Mrs. Schultz was—at the very beginning to make the connection for her, but Papa could simply have driven to Acton and telephoned Mrs. Schultz. She charged two dollars for a treatment when you went to her home, one dollar for an absent treatment—which was a lot different from the hundreds we had had to shell out for the appendix operation. After Mamma really understood how to Know the Truth, she would not need the practitioner. She could study the weekly lesson or—so Mrs. Schultz had told her—simply open up *Science and Health* and put her finger down on a page at random. Nine times out of ten, *there* would be the appropriate text to purge the body of pain and the mind of doubt.

I don't think that Papa ever quite understood it, but he went along with it. He said if it worked it would be a hell of a lot better to get right through to The Head Man than try to persuade some highway robber of a sawbones to come twenty miles when you needed him. And, he speculated, if He could prevent accidents and cure up diseases, how about disasters of nature?

Mamma, the instant authority, said there was nothing too small or too big to ask of Him. "Get to work on hailstorms," Papa said.

Mamma did. She thought it would be selfish merely to ask God to detour His hail around our fields, so she asked Him to protect the whole rim while He was at it. I don't think she went so far as to suggest that He hold off on hail completely—there must be some Divine Plan in everything that happened and she would not presume to interfere with that—but merely to navigate such omnipotent destruction down south of the rim, where practically nobody lived.

Unfortunately, she forgot to mention drought to Him. Or maybe only Indians could intercede for rain, and they were not doing any dances for the white man who had taken their land away from them and cooped them up on the Crow Reservation.

The Chinook turned on a little late that spring. There was almost no snow for it to melt by then, so it merely sucked up what little moisture was frozen in the topsoil.

Jim Harper quit his dishwashing job at the Commercial and came back to us in time to rake the field where the winter wheat had been sown, but he was changed somehow. Less of a boy and more of a man. He had met a girl in Billings. She was a half-breed, and he was touchy enough about that, but that was only part of it. Her name was Fern Sparks. Whenever we had company Papa would say, "Tell them what your girl's name is, Jim," Jim would stammer and hem and haw, and finally say, "Fern Sparks." The inevitable farmyard comment on that was always, "Oh, she does, does she?" Jim could never think of an adequate comeback to that one, so he would blush to the roots of his hair and everybody would laugh.

Once he brought Fern out to meet us. We were the only family Jim had, and he wanted to show his girl that he was not just a fly-by-night dishwasher but somebody well regarded by substantial landholders like the Eunsons. I suspect he had puffed us up in the telling because she did not have much to say when he showed her around the place.

Fern was a disappointment to me. She looked like any other girl in shirtwaist and saddle skirt, no more like an

Indian than Genevieve. She wore her hair piled high on her head and held her sailor hat on with a hatpin. There was something incongruous to me in an Indian girl—even a half-Indian girl—wearing a hatpin. It was a far cry from a tomahawk.

She wanted to see where Jim lived, and he was about to take her out and show her the bunkhouse when Mamma said politely, "Jim, be sure to show Fern your bearskin."

Jim said, "Yes, ma'am, that's what I'm aiming to do," and then we noticed the girl's face, and Mamma realized what she had said. She started to laugh—she had not laughed much since she had been in Science—and then made it worse by saying to the girl, "I didn't mean that. I meant his bear hide." Then she couldn't stop laughing to explain any further, and it was probably just as well. Jim led the girl out and Mamma sank into her rocking chair, holding her side where she had had the operation.

The seasons began to repeat themselves. Spring stretched out the days and warmed the sun, the still unbroken prairie flamed with bitterroot and wild roses and cactus, the white-tailed antelopes dropped their fawns, and the wolves and coyotes their pups. Overhead the wild geese honked their way north, late this year, and once more it was time for planning and planting the vegetable garden and for the south half of section 33 to be plowed for sowing in the fall.

Each morning we would stare at the western sky for a hint of rain clouds. Sometimes they would pile up over the Crazies like mounds of whipped egg whites, but few of them dared that dehydrating voyage across the plain and the few that did jealously guarded their moisture. At evening the dry blue blanket of the sky was once more tucked in around the mountains for the night.

April arrived, but no April showers. We lugged water to sprout the seeds in the garden—the water level in our well was still not affected by the drought—but there was no way to get it to the wheat field. Uncle Charlie wrote to ask how the crop was coming along and Mamma had to respond, "No sign of it yet. The seed just lies there. We better get rain within a few days or the growing season will be too short."

Then the wind roared and picked up stinging dust out of the parched fields around us. We rode out to section 33 and watched our rich topsoil blowing away in a dirty, earthbound cloud, across Henry Williams's and Earl Hickson's homesteads and then down the eastern slope of the rim, never to return.

"I shouldn't have told Jim to rake that field," Papa said. "That might have helped some."

The hail last year, a drought this year. It began to look, even to the most optimistic homesteader, as if you could not depend on the gentle rains from heaven upon the earth beneath to make you rich. You'd better diversify if you hoped to survive. Then you might be able to afford to wait for that big, perfect year to produce the bumper crop, the all but mythical sixty bushels to the acre.

Papa went to Billings and brought back twenty yearlings to fatten. We would pasture them on the south half of the homestead, which had never been plowed and was not worth plowing, and sell them this fall. He also bought an incubator, for which space was made in the corner beside the piano. It was not what you'd call pretty, but at least it covered up Molly's hoofprint, Mamma said. She was bored with that as a conversation piece.

The incubator's tray held 144 eggs—a square of twelve each way. It was heated by its own kerosene lamp, and the temperature of the thermometer that lay on the eggs must be held at 103 degrees for the three weeks it took to hatch out a batch of baby chicks. Beneath the tray we set a pan of water to keep the air moist. The eggs had to be hand-turned twice a day. Otherwise the developing embryos would stick to the shells and die.

Turning the eggs—we put a penciled cross on one side—became my duty, but I never found it tedious or onerous because inside each one of them was occurring the incredible miracle of the creation of life.

Mamma would lift out the tray and put it on the table for the turning, which must be accomplished quickly, before the egg temperature fell more than a couple degrees. Then she would set the tray back. At the end of ten days we tested each egg for its fertility. By that time, when you held an egg before the flame of a candle, the blood vessels of the chick developing out of the yolk and albumen should turn the egg opaque instead of translucent. The room had to be dark, of course. If you could still see light through an egg you had to throw it out. The egg was not fertile and soon would rot. A rotten egg inside an incubator could kill the embryos near it. There were usually five or six bad ones to a setting.

Along about the nineteenth day the suspense grew unbearable. Which egg would hatch first? How many baby chicks would there be? Observation of the process was less than adequate through the little glass window in the tray door, but it was better than trying to watch under a setting hen. A setting hen, I had discovered last year, got very cross if you lifted her off her nest at that stage of the game. You'd better wear thick gloves. But the hen was right, of course. A chill blast of air on the egg at that vital period could kill the chick.

I must have looked through that door forty times a day so as not to miss the sight of that first little yellow bill breaking through. On the morning of the twenty-first day Mamma warmed up the room and then lifted the tray out and gingerly set it on the table. I leaned over it and could actually hear sounds coming from inside the eggs—the weak pecking for release and a few faint peeps.

And then, as I carefully turned an egg, it cracked right under my eyes. For a moment I was afraid I had done it. Then something moved. A triangle of eggshell fell away and there was the yellow bill gasping its first breath. I screamed for Mamma.

She stared at it for a long moment and then for some reason wiped her eyes with her apron. "And some folks don't believe in God the Creator," she said.

"It's dying," I said, staring at the gasping beak. "We better help it out."

"No," Mamma said. "That would kill it. Birth takes a long time. The little thing's got to rest awhile now and get stronger. Then it'll go at it again."

She slid the tray back into the incubator and closed the door. All that day—fortunately it was a Saturday—I knelt on the floor, with my eyes staring through the little glass door.

By evening there were—among the clutter of stained eggshells—114 baby chicks in various stages of drying, ready to be taken out and put in the brooder. It was, everybody said, a pretty good percentage to hatch out of the 138 eggs that had been left after the candling. If we raised seventy or eighty we could consider ourselves lucky.

Next day we cleaned the eggshells out of the tray. scrubbed it, and loaded the incubator all over again.

"SHEP TOLD ME."

Nineteen

Finally a few showers fell between Broadview and Belmont. Now that the soil up there was moist, Harry Gullard hired himself out to run a tractor. On the way to school—Selma and I were both walking because the Gullard horses were needed at home and Fly was getting too heavy to ride; her stomach squeaked when she trotted—Selma boasted that her brother was knocking down four dollars a day. Naturally I told her she was lying. Nobody that I knew to talk to could possibly make money like that. When I told Papa, he was almost as dubious as I had been, but next time we saw old Chris he confirmed it. "Dot Harry," he said, wheezing a bit, "he yust make anyt'ing to work, and folks'll pay him for it."

Papa told Mr. Gullard that if it was all the same to him he was not going to mention this to Jim Harper. Jim might think he could do as well, but he did not have a knack with machinery. It would just make him more itchy, and he was itchy enough as it was over that half-breed girl.

It seemed as if Jim spent all his spare time writing to Fern. Writing came hard for him, and he wanted to impress her because her father had been a teacher on the reservation—that's how Fern's parents had met—and Fern herself wrote a beautiful, precise hand. Sometimes Jim would ask Mamma to read his letters before he mailed them, just to make sure they were spelled correctly and his mistakes in grammar were not too glaring. Mamma told Papa that they didn't seem much like love letters to her— Jim told Fern about how late the crops were and how we needed rain and how Mr. Eunson had bought a couple Duroc-Jersey brood sows. The nearest he came to anything personal was an account of how Carl Gullard was teaching him to roll a coffin nail with one hand even when he was on horseback and the wind blowing. When Jim had that down pat he would ride to Billings some Sunday and show off to her.

That and how I claimed I could understand what Shep was trying to say. He wondered if Fern thought there could be anything in that? (When he asked her a question, he figured she would answer his letters quicker.)

Mamma finished reading and correcting that letter and told him it was very nice except she thought "Yours truly" was a bit formal for a personal letter, and why didn't he change it to "Sincerely" at least. But when he was gone to make the change she said in a solemn voice, "Dale, you oughtn't to tell Jim things like that."

I told her that was what Miss Moody had said. Miss Moody told me I shouldn't tell anybody, but lately Jim was so hard to talk to, I was only trying to think of something that would catch his interest and it had slipped out.

"Miss Moody told you you shouldn't tell anybody *what?*"

"About me and Shep," I explained.

I went on about how Miss Moody had found out about it and said we had better keep it a secret.

Mamma didn't say anything but simply stood there looking at me, so I asked her if she would promise not to tell anybody. If she told, somebody might steal Shep and put him in the circus, or maybe steal us both, because I was the only one who could understand him. I might have to interpret for him, the way the Polish man had to interpret for Ignatz.

"You must not tell lies like that," Mamma finally said.

"But I'm *not* telling lies. I do understand him."

"We all understand dogs more or less, because dogs are very simple creatures with simple needs that they express simply," Mamma said. "But we do not understand everything that goes on in their heads, because they do not think in words the way humans do."

"Shep does," I said.

Mamma said I'd better stop talking such nonsense and practice my Clementi, but before I could get to the piano stool she changed her mind. She was standing at the screen door looking down at Shep, who was tied to one of the posts of the stoop. "Come here, Dale," she said. She pointed at Shep. "Very well. What is he thinking right now?"

Shep cocked his watch-eye at me and whined. It was almost too easy. "He's saying, 'Let me loose so I can go see that lady coyote.'"

"*Shep Told Me.*"

Mamma sucked in her breath. "How did you know about the lady coyote?" she gasped.

"Shep told me," I said.

I had to say that because if I told the rest of it she would think I was merely making up Shep's thoughts on the subject, and I wasn't. That's exactly what he was thinking at the time. But a couple days before Mamma had told me that we were going to keep Shep tied to the clothesline for a few days to try to keep him from following me to school. That same day I overheard Papa and Jim talking in the barn. Jim said that Peterson had told him there was a coyote bitch in heat somewhere on the rim and we'd better keep our dog tied up if we didn't want the rest of her beaus to rip him to shreds.

If I told Mamma that, she would be mad at Papa for not noticing I was around when he and Jim were talking men's talk. Besides, then she would know that I knew she had lied to me. Mamma and Papa really didn't care whether Shep followed me to school or not because he wasn't any good for anything else anyhow. They'd both said that many times.

"I'm going to have to talk to your father," Mamma said. "And in the meantime I don't want to hear one more word about Shep talking to anybody!" She straightened her apron. "Now then. Let's see how fast we can get through Clementi Number One without stumbling."

Papa and Mamma must have done their talking where I could not overhear them. Papa never mentioned it, and Mamma kept mum after that too. Then one Sunday night—it was April 14—I was informed that I was going to Billings next day with Mamma. The doctor had made her promise to return for a checkup around the middle of April. Mamma said she would let the doctor check her up if it would make him feel any better, but personally she thought it was a waste of time and money. She was in Science now, and God's perfect child did not need checkups.

I should have been suspicious, Monday being a school day and all, but I did not question my luck because we were going to travel from Acton by train and would stay at the Commercial Hotel that night. I would get to see Genevieve and eat chop suey at the Chinese restaurant up the marble stairs and look in windows at the shiny new automobiles.

We arrived a little before noon and registered at the hotel so we could get rid of our grips. Then we walked up Montana Avenue, but we ran into a thousand sheep being driven to the stockyards for shipment to Chicago and we had to climb the library steps to get out of their way.

But finally we made it to Twenty-eighth Street and turned north toward Hart-Albin's where Genevieve worked. Mamma needed a new shirtwaist and a skirt and Genevieve could get 20 percent discounts.

It made me proud to watch my sister doing her job. She was no longer a clerk but had a very important position making change for all the baskets that zoomed at her from every corner of the bargain basement. It did not seem to fluster her at all. Mamma and I stood there quite a while before she even had time to look up. When she finally spotted us, she did not smile. That was odd, because Genevieve was always happy to see us—even Mamma. It took her a few minutes to remember that she and Mamma didn't get along.

As soon as she could she got another girl to take her

place. Then she stepped down out of the cage and kissed us both and asked after Papa. Mamma asked her if she could come out for a bite to eat with us somehwere, and Genevieve said she simply did not feel like eating.

Mamma said she hoped she wasn't coming down with the grippe that was going around, and Genevieve said no, it wasn't that, it was the thought of all those poor souls.

"What poor souls?" Mamma asked.

"You mean you haven't heard about the *Titanic*?" Genevieve gasped.

No, Mamma said. What about the *Titanic*?

"It hit an iceberg and sank. Nobody knows yet whether anybody at all was saved."

Mamma turned white and had to sit down. Genevieve got her a glass of water and I said if I had a paper I would fan her. But there was no newspaper today. It was Monday and the *Gaxette* did not publish on Mondays. That was the reason we had been able to walk all the way from the Northern Pacific station to Hart-Albin's without hearing newsboys crying "Extra." But as the Associated Press dispatches on the disaster were received over the Morse circuit, they were pasted on the bulleting board outside the *Gaxette* office.

Even a boy not quite eight years old living on a homestead in Montana knew all about the *Titanic*. There had been stories about her in the Milwaukee *Sentinel* that Uncle Charlie mailed to us every once in a while. She was the biggest thing afloat, probably the biggest ship that ever *would* be built, certainly the most luxurious, and claims had been made that she was unsinkable. And here, on her maiden voyage, laden with celebrities, she had gone to the bottom. If any of the twenty-four hundred aboard had been saved it would be a miracle.

After a little while Mamma managed to pull herself together. She felt in no mood for shopping, but "Life must go on," she said, and bought herself a new corset as well as the skirt and shirtwaist. I could hardly pull myself away from a pair of tan oxfords with brass toe-snubbers. Genevieve wanted to buy them for me, but Mamma wouldn't let her. They were dangerous, she said; a boy needed high-toppers when he lived in rattlesnake country. So Genevieve gave us a leather pillow with a picture of Teddy Roosevelt staring out across the ocean burned on it. Under it the caption read, WHAT ARE THE WILD WAVES SAYING? THIRD TERM. Hart-Albin's had stocked the pillows because Teddy Roosevelt was stumping through town soon in his campaign against President Taft for the Republican nomination.

The shopping had made everbody feel better, so Genevieve decided to come out and have something to eat after all, especially since she could not have supper with us; she had a previous engagement.

We all ordered clubhouse sandwiches, even though they cost thirty-five cents apiece. Genevieve said it was her treat. She was sorry she could not spend the evening with us but she had had this previous engagement for two weeks and could not very well cancel it at this late date. If she had only known we were coming to Billings . . .

Mamma said that did not matter at all. She and I would think of something exciting to do by ourselves. What was playing at the Babcock?

"*Uncle Tom's Cabin,*" Genevieve said.

Mamma had seen that in Milwaukee years ago, but she thought I ought to be exposed to it if it wasn't too dear. It was like an American history lesson.

Genevieve said the third balcony usually cost seventy-five cents; that is, if Mamma was up to the climb after her operation. Mamma said she wouldn't even tell the doctor about it when she saw him. It was none of his business. We would go if we could get tickets.

We were having a good time. Nobody was mad at anybody, and then Genevieve put her foot in it. She had gone to the Babcock only last Thursday, she said. She and a new beau who was a real swell sat in the orchestra and they had seen Mrs. Leslie Carter in *Two Women*.

"Mrs. Leslie Carter was right here in Billings and you didn't let me know?" Mamma cut in.

"I didn't know she was a friend of yours," Genevieve said, tightening up.

She was not a friend, Mamma said, but she had seen her in Chicago when she was playing in *The Heart of Maryland* and she would never forget it. Mrs. Carter had clung to the clapper of a big bell and swung right out over the audience.

"Why?" Genevieve said, flat. It seemed to me a reasonable question.

"Because if the bell rang," Mamma said, and turned to me as if *I* had asked, "that was to be the signal that her sweetheart was to be executed. I'll never forget it," she repeated.

I could easily understand that. It was something one would not easily forget. Then Mamma turned back to Genevieve and said sadly, "And so Mrs. Leslie Carter was here last Thursday, and you didn't tell me. We could have made this trip then just as well as today."

Genevieve said she was sorry. If she had known how Mamma felt about Mrs. Carter she would have gone out of her way to tell her. But, she went on, *Two Women* was hardly appropriate fare for a seven-year-old-boy, and besides, Mrs. Carter did not swing out over the audience on any bell last Thursday. "We sat in the fourth row and I would certainly have noticed a thing like that," she said.

A long silence followed, and then Genevieve asked for the check. There was an embarrassing moment while she looked in her coin purse and discovered she did not have enough cash to pay the tab, but Mamma came to the rescue by lending her fifty cents. "I'll leave the money at the hotel tomorrow morning on my way to work," Genevieve said grimly.

"No need," Mamma said.

"Oh, yes, there is," Genevieve persisted. "I said it was my treat, and it is my treat!"

So far that day we had suffered two disasters: the *Titanic* and Mrs. Leslie Carter.

"ARE YOU GENTLEMEN IN THE MARKET FOR A FORD?"

Twenty

"The doctor says I'm fit as a fiddle," Mamma said as she came out of his office. But then, she went on smugly, he did not have to tell her that; she knew it already. And it was none of his doing that she was so well. That was because of God and Mrs. Eddy and Mrs. Schultz and the Scientific Statement of Being.

"And where are we going now?" I asked her as we boarded a streetcar.

"To see Mrs. Schultz," Mamma said mysteriously.

Mrs. Schultz lived with two fat calico cats in a small, two-story house out Division Street way. She was as fat as her cats, still limped, and used a cane. She was older than

Mamma and her glasses dangled from a gold chain that pulled out of a *fleur de lis* pod pinned to the blouse of her dress. She seemed happy to see Mamma and me, though it was hard to tell whether a person was happy or sad when she smiled all the time.

Mamma said she needed some help, so I played with the cats—Mrs. Schultz told us they were named Katz and Jammer for the funny paper's Katzenjammer Kids—while the two ladies retired to the treatment room. After about twenty minutes Mamma returned and told me that Mrs. Schultz would like to see me.

"What for?" I wanted to know.

"Don't ask questions," Mamma said.

One of the cats followed and jumped up on me after Mrs. Schultz sat me down in a chair opposite her. "I think I'd better take Jammer," she said, and set him in her lap, patted him on the head and scratched him behind the ears. He began to purr audibly.

The walls were covered with wallpaper plastered with fading cabbage roses. Massive ferns banked the bay window that framed Mrs. Schultz. She sat in a rocker with her cat but did not rock. "Do you know how lucky you are to have a mamma like yours?" she finally asked.

"Yeah, I know," I told her. Because it was true, I did know.

And did I know how concerned my wonderful mamma had been over me lately?

I hedged on that one. "What about?"

"Your doggie," she said. "About your insisting you can understand what your doggie is thinking about."

"But I *can*," *I* told her. I wanted to add "And he isn't anybody's doggie!" because if there was one thing Shep couldn't stand it was being called a doggie. But it was disrespectful for a child to correct adults.

"We *think* we can," Mrs. Schultz said, "and sometimes thinking makes it seem so to us."

"I don't think—I know," I said.

"Well. That's neither here nor there." Mrs. Schultz scratched Jammer behind the ear. "We are not to worry about it any more."

"I'm not worried about it now," I told her.

"Mm-hmm," she said. "Let's both be very still for a little while. Just don't think about anything at all."

She opened her copy of *Science and Health*. Its markers for the weekly lesson made it bristle like a scared porcupine. She did not read from it but held it in her lap on top of the purring Jammer and then turned and looked out the window through the ferns. She must have had her mind on something else because she didn't even notice that Jammer was chewing on a marker.

I tried to sit still, but the chair was hard and I kept thinking about going back downtown where things were going on. It didn't seem fair, after being up on the rim all winter, to come to town and have to spend the afternoon with a funny old lady who held a cat and a book on her lap and smiled and mumbled and stared out the window.

And then it suddenly came to me what Mrs. Schultz was up to. She was trying to fix it with God so I could not understand Shep any more. Well, I said to myself, she's got another think coming!

Finally she came out of her trance. I was permitted to get off the chair at last and follow her into the front room where Mamma was deep in the *Christian Science Sentinel*.

Mrs. Schultz patted my head the way she had patted Jammer's. Next thing you know she's going to scratch me behind the ears, I thought. "We're fine now," she said to Mamma, "but if we experience any more manifestations of mortal error, just let us know." I knew who *we* were, because that was the way a schoolteacher talked—not Miss Moody, but Miss Freeman and one I had had back in Neillsville. But I was not so sure about *us*. *Us* probably meant Mrs. Schultz and God.

Mamma paid her four dollars—two for herself and two for me—and we said goodbye.

I did not feel any different, but I could hardly wait to get home and test out whether I could still talk with Shep or not.

We got off the streetcar in front of the Babcock and Mamma bought two tickets for *Uncle Tom's Cabin*. Then she went to the hotel to get out of her high heels and corset and lie down for a while. She was not used to walking on cement sidewalks and it tired her. She let me go for a walk. I headed straight for the Ford automobile display. There was a real whizzer in the window—its brass radiator and headlamps glistening, its leather straps, guaranteed to keep the top from blowing off, clamped to the front fenders.

While I stood lalligagging at it somebody touched me on the shoulder. I turned to look up into Uncle Corve's face. I yelled "Uncle Corve!" and hugged him, and then we shook hands formally. He had driven to Billings alone this morning to buy a mule, but before he started for home he wanted to take a look at the automobile here in the show window. He had seen pictures of it in the *Saturday Evening Post*—but "I never really touched a live one," he said.

"Let's go in and look at it up close," I said.

Uncle Corve took a quick glance around as if to see if anybody was spying on us, then he took my hand and led me in. "The kid here," he said to the salesman, "wants to take a squint at your Tin Lizzie."

"He can look to his heart's content," the salesman said. "Are you gentlemen in the market for a Ford?"

Again that quick look around. "I'm studyin' it," Uncle Corve said. "How much does this one set you back?"

"This one," the salesman said reverently, "you can drive right out of here for three hundred and eighty-five dollars. I sold one just like it to the mayor only last week."

We must have stayed there half an hour, looking under the hood, jouncing the springs, and kicking the hard, smooth tires. When we left—Uncle Corve finally took a look at his watch—I said, "You were just kidding when you said you were studyin' buying one of those, weren't you, Uncle Corve?"

"Maybe yes, maybe no," Uncle Corve said with a last glance back at the showroom. "I might kick over the traces one o' these days. But don't let on to your ma. She'd blab to Edie, and Edie'd probably put the kibosh on it. If I do it, I'm just going to do it and surprise her."

"I won't tell anybody," I said. "But how do you reckon Aunt Edie's going to take to being surprised?"

Uncle Corve grinned. "Hell," he said, "that's no skin off my teeth." He was whistling in the dark, of course, and he knew it. Aunt Edie had a temper and wasn't afraid to let it out.

I told Mamma I had run into Uncle Corve, but I said it was in front of Yegen Brothers instead of the Ford salesroom.

After a chop suey supper we walked over to the Babcock where we were directed around to the alley. There we climbed the outside stairs to the third balcony. Mamma had to stop to get her breath at each level—she said it was because the new corset was laced too tight—but we finally made it. The balcony was so high that we seemed to hang right over the stage, and the declension so steep there was room for but four or five rows of benches. The man and woman behind us seemed to be standing on our shoulders, but when the lights were lowered and the curtain went up I forgot all that.

Mamma whispered that it was not a very good company compared with some she had seen, but I suspect that was because the benches were so hard. (The smart customers had brought pillows.) So far as I was concerned, nothing could have been more wondrous. When it came to the scene of Simon Legree and the bloodhounds chasing Eliza across the ice, my breath stuck in my chest. At first blush the ice, from our aerie, looked like wooden blocks on a dirty canvas, but presently it defied all evidence of our eyes and turned to ice floating on water into which the poor woman would surely slip and fall to her death.

Mamma tried not to cry, but she could no more help herself than I when Little Eva ascended toward heaven and disappeared behind the proscenium arch of the Babcock.

We were still sniffling when we came out onto the iron stairs leading to the alley below and found that rain was pouring down. The other patrons from the balcony must have thought we were crazy because we simply stood there and let it rain on us. By the time we made it down the last flight we were drenched, but who cared?

If it was raining like this up on the rim, then the wheat, or some of it at any rate, would sprout at last!

It rained hard all night, but the sun was bright and the brick pavement steaming in the morning when we went to the station. Mamma bought a copy of the Tuesday, April 16, Billings *Gazette* with the awful headline about the *Titanic:* 1500 GO DOWN TO DEATH IN THE SEA. On such a sunny day in Montana, that seemed like a remote Martian happening. Then Mamma came to an item about Ole Abelseth, a Norwegian who lived in Columbus, which was only about thirty-five miles or so west of Acton. Mr. Abelseth had been returning on the *Titanic* from a visit to the old country and was presumed lost.

That brought it right home to Mamma. "Why, it might have been Chris Gullard!" she exclaimed.

"How come?" I asked.

"Well, he's Norwegian too. If he had gone back to Lillehammer to pay a visit to his relatives, he probably would have been coming home on the *Titanic* the way Ole Abelseth was."

"I hadn't thought of it that way, Mamma," I said.

We were both awed to silence for a few moments by the narrow escape our good neighbor Chris Gullard had had. Then Mamma wiped her eyes and looked at the next headline: RAIN BREAKS DROUGHT!

"The Lord giveth and the Lord taketh away," she said.

There was no doubt about the rain being general. The farther we got from Billings, the harder it had rained. Between Mossmain and Hesper a cloudburst had washed out a trestle. Our train ground to a halt and we all piled out of the coaches lugging our grips. We had to slip and slide down a steep and muddy embankment and step from rock to rock across the gully where water still trickled. "Just like Eliza!" Mamma cried gaily.

Then we scrambled up the opposite bank to the track where another train awaited us. Nobody grumbled about the inconvenience because most of the passengers were dryland farmers who would have walked a hundred miles across burning sands barefoot if that would have guaranteed rain.

It had rained at last, and rain meant new clothes to take the place of those you had been making do with, a fresh roast of beef and white bread once in a while instead of the ubiquitous salt pork and johnnycake and potatoes, a filling for that cavity in your tooth next time you went to Billings (you were going to have something to sell this fall, so the merchants and dentists would give you more credit, even before the harvest) . But most of all it meant your father could pay up, or shrink, the debt at the bank. When your father was in debt to the bank, there was a load on his shoulders that he could never quite straighten up under. He didn't talk much about it because what good did talking do? But it was there. His voice did not carry quite as far when he first spotted you coming home from school and called out, he sometimes didn't hear what Mamma was saying to him, and he didn't jump quite so high at square dances.

Rain would change all that.

Papa was waiting for us when the train stopped at Acton. He was grinning, and he took Mamma and hugged her and swung her clear up off the ground. Mamma pretended to be provoked with him: "Careful, Robert! My shoes! I'll never be able to scrape the gumbo off them!"

"The hell with your shoes!" he cried. "Throw the damn things away. We can buy new ones now."

"Are You Gentlemen in the Market for a Ford?" 175

We had been gone for only twenty-four hours, but it seemed like a month. It seemed strange that things still looked about the same. The only difference was that the wind was not kicking up any dust.

"Where's Shep?" I asked.

Mamma and Papa exchanged glances. "I left him to home," Papa said. "The train might've run over him."

"Tied up? He could get tangled in the rope and choke to death."

"No. He's locked in the barn," Papa said.

We had lots of news to tell—about the *Titanic*, of course, and seeing Genevieve, and *Uncle Tom's Cabin*, and me running into Uncle Corve, and what the doctor had said about Mamma's being fit as a fiddle, and Mrs. Schultz, "She gave me a treatment . . . I think," I told Papa.

"Oh?" Papa said.

So he was in on it. If he had not known why Mamma took me he would have asked what for, because I wasn't sick or anything. That was why they had kept me out of school to go to Billings, I suddenly realized.

"Everything's going to be . . . all right," Mamma said, "from now on. It was only a manifestation of error."

"Is that a fact?" Papa said. When he said it like that Mamma could not accuse him of being a skeptic. He was merely saying, in his own way, "I'll wait and see."

He did not have long to wait. When we got home I ran to the barn to let Shep out but he wasn't there. Jim, who was splitting wood, stopped and explained that he had heard an unholy ruckus from the chicken yard, and when he went to investigate, there was Shep in the middle of it. He had worried the catch loose on the door between the barn and the coop, then wormed his way through the chickens' twelve-inch opening into the year, and had killed our biggest rooster.

"What did you do with him?" Mamma asked.

"Whacked him good and shut him in the bunkhouse," Jim said.

I ran to the bunkhouse and opened the door, which was pretty badly scratched where shep had been trying to get out. He was not at all ashamed of what he had done. He jumped and frisked and licked my face. I was almost afraid to ask him why he had done what he did for fear I couldn't understand him any longer, but I finally said, "Shep, why in tarnation did you kill the rooster?" and he came back with, "I *had* to because the old devil had caught one of the hens and was standing on her."

I had never gone so far as to kill the rooster when I found him chasing the hens, but I had thrown rocks at him. Once I asked Papa why we didn't eat him for dinner some Sunday when Aunt Edie and Uncle Corve came over. Roosters were too tough, Papa said. Then what were they good for, I asked? They were company for the hens, Papa said, and crowed them awake in the morning so they could get to work laying eggs early.

I had figured on the way home that if I could still understand Shep I wouldn't mention it. They might take me back to Mrs. Schultz, and next time she might bring it off. But this made everything different. I had to explain the Mamma and Papa that Shep had a good reason for doing what he did, or they would get rid of him.

We both tore back to the house and I repeated what Shep had told me. Jim's face turned red, and he excused himself and said he'd better finish chopping wood. Mamma slapped her forehead with her hand, shut her eyes, and

Knew the Truth for a minute, and then said, "Dale, what in the world are we going to do?"

"He won't do it again," I said, "as long as we don't have an ugly old rooster around."

"I mean with you lying like a trooper all the time," she said, and walked in the house to unpack, while Papa and I went down to the barn to unharness the horses.

When that was done, Papa said he guessed it was time he explained about the rooster and the hens. What he said did not make much sense to me, but if Papa said it, then it must be so.

"Just the same," I said, "you can't blame Shep for trying to protect the hens. Nobody's told him about things like that."

"Then, by Jeezlum, you'd better tell him!" Papa said. Then I guess he realized what he had said, because he laughed and slapped his thigh. "Next thing, you'll have me believing it!" he said.

We had the rooster for supper, even though it was only Tuesday. Sunday was chicken day, but this one would not keep, even in the root cellar, till Sunday. There had been no teethmarks on him—Shep had just grabbed him and wrung his neck, the way he'd seen Papa and Jim do when they killed chickens.

Maybe what Papa had told me about roosters was true, crazy as it sounded, but this Don Juan was a tough old customer as well. Nobody complimented Mamma on her fricassee that night.

"IF IT GETS TOO ROUGH, COME AND TALK TO ME."

Twenty-One

The early spring winds had blown about half the seed plumb out of the ground, Papa said, after inspecting the field that was beginning to green up in patches, and the heavy rain, which had arrived in the nick of time, had carved striae through the soil of the slopes. Papa had learned his lesson. Next year he would go in for that new-fangled contour plowing which was supposed to help keep excess water from running off.

We would be lucky if we got twenty or twenty-five bushels to the acre this year, which was quite a letdown after last fall's tall talk of forty or fifty. Papa allowed as how he had been a little overoptimistic. But byGodandbyJesus, he was glad he had been, because it had kept his spirits up during the winter. Counting all that mazuma sure as hell beat counting sheep for putting you to sleep—especially when you were in debt.

Anyhow, he would not turn up his nose at twenty or twenty-five bushels, Papa said, mulling it over. Three hundred and twenty acres, well, let's say twenty-five bushels until the actual count makes a damn liar out of us—320 times 25 is, let's see, what does that come to? You're good at arithmetic, Jessie, you used to be a schoolteacher, what does that come out to? Eight thousand, you say? Can that be right? Yep. Eight thousand. A nice round figure like yours, Mamma. Now say the price of wheat stays steady at seventy-five cents, that's six thousand. Not bad. A lot better than a swift kick in the pants!

The bank loan could be lifted, we'd pay Uncle Charlie a big installment on section 33, and there'd be oodles left over.

"For you know what," Mamma said to Papa with a significant lift of her eyebrows.

When you are seven-years-old-going-on-eight, time moves like a drowsy caterpillar. Days are weeks, weeks months, and months years. I would swear on a stack of Bibles that it was two years between the middle of April 1912 and the time school let out the middle of June. Nothing happened but growth—of cattle, pigs, chickens, horses, crops. The sun came up in the morning and went down a week or so later. Meadowlarks sang and nested in the buffalo grass, and rattlesnakes shed their skins and added another rattler to their warning signal. Weeds grew faster than the vegetables in the garden and had to be rousted out.

Having been denied rain for so long, now, when it was

almost too late, we had more than enough and no way to conserve what we did not need. There was talk of mildew, of rust, of a plague of grasshoppers. When there was nothing palpable for a dryland farmer to worry about, he had to invent ominous intangibles to populate his nightmares.

None of these things would come to pass, Mamma announced with complete conviction. She read her lesson every morning after the dishes were done and the hogs slopped, and she Knew the Truth all day. I guess she figured she had all natural phenomena under firm control, at least on the rim. Even Shep managed to creep in under the benign umbrella of her drag with the Almighty. There had been talk of "giving him to some little fellow whose family doesn't keep chickens," but I guess the sight of my stricken face had been too much for Mamma and Papa. Shep was going to be allowed one more chance to shape up as God's Perfect Dog.

But there was a subtle change in Mamma herself, and it was confusing. I never knew what mood she would be in when she got up in the morning. Little things got her goat. If the Blodgetts came to call, they didn't know when it was time to leave; if they failed to stop by occasionally, they were not good neighbors.

It seemed as if I could not please her either. When I was noisy and rambunctious, I was doing it to interfere with her meditations; when I kept quiet, it was unnatural for a normal boy to be that quiet. What was I up to?

Then sometimes for no reason at all, so far as I could judge, she would suddenly clasp me to her and hug me and tell me that I was hers just as much as if she'd borned me. Once I heard her heart beating—loud. It was the first time I ever heard a heart beat, and it was terrifying. I pushed away from her and ran down to the well for a drink of cold water. Shep followed me.

A tin dipper hung on the pump. I pumped it full of water and drank as much as I could, then offered the rest to Shep, who was thirsty too. I knew he was not supposed to drink out of our dipper, but that did not make much sense to me. People were always saying a thing was clean as a hound's tooth. Anyhow, I was going to rinse out the dipper after he finished.

But suddenly Mamma was there, flailing the air with the fly swatter because the dampness had bred a vicious crop of mosquitoes. How many times had I been told not to let Shep drink out of the dipper? *(Swat.)* What was she going to do? *(Swat, swat!)* She was at her wit's end to cope with me. *Why* had I done it? *(Swat, swat, swat!)*

I hesitated and then said, "I don't know," because I'd found out that "I don't know," while not the truth, was the shortest course out of a situation. Mamma's retort to that was usually, "Of course you know," and then I'd say, "Well, I'm sorry," and she would say, "You *should* be," and pretty soon such stupid conversation was too boring for her to pursue, and she would say, "I give up," and go back to whatever she had been doing.

Today, however, that gambit did not pay off. "That's a silly thing to say and you know it!" Mamma said. "It's just as big a fib as if you had lied outright and said, `Because Shep told me he was thirsty.' "

"I wasn't going to say that," I said.

"But it's what he was thinking, is that it?"

"He wasn't even thinking it."

"That's another lie, isn't it? Because he *was* thinking it." She was shouting now, and neither of us really knew what we were saying.

"All right," I yelled. "He was thinking it! Is that what you want me to say?"

I began to back away, because Mamma's face was getting red and splotched, and she looked as if she wanted to shake me. I wasn't sure I could outrun her, or that it wouldn't be worse for me in the end if I could. I glanced around for Papa but he was nowhere in sight. And then, just as she was about to make a grab for me, she sat down on the pump platform and began to cry. Not gently, but with great wracking, heaving sobs. She was mumbling something between sobs, but the only thing I could make out was "God help me. I made him say that."

"I'll go get Papa," I said.

"No . . . no, don't," she said and looked up at me. Her eyes were red and her cheeks tear-stained.

"What's the matter, Mamma?" I finally managed to ask.

She did not answer but stared off for a long while, up through the draw toward the Gullards'. Finally she heaved a sigh and said, "I'm sorry."

Mamma had never said that before. It seemed wrong somehow. A child is sorry when he has done wrong, but a parent should always be right and never have anything to apologize for. The devil walked over my grave.

"What've you got to be sorry for, Mamma?" I asked, trying to keep my teeth from chattering.

I guess she didn't hear me, because she did not answer. After a minute or two she got up, squared her shoulders, and looked down at the old fly swatter that had seen better days. "Remind me to write 'Fly swatter' on the list next time we go to Robinson's store," she said, and walked off toward the house.

In a little while I found Papa cleaning the manure out of

the barn. He could tell something was the matter and asked me what it was. I said I couldn't tell him because it would be like tattling.

"Who have you got to tattle on?" he asked.

"I can't tell," I said, because he had told me once that when Mamma said a thing, that was *it* and not to come running to him.

After a minute he said, "If it's about Mamma, you better tell me."

"But you said . . . ."

"I know," he said, "but your mamma's not feeling very good, and we mustn't pay too much attention to what she does these days."

Not pay much attention to what Mamma does? That was shaking the ground under my feet. "Is she sick again?"

"Yes . . . and no," he said. "It's hard to explain."

"You mean she's sick in the head?"

"No no. Nothing like that."

"Is she maybe not over the operation yet?"

Papa stared at me for quite a while, and I knew he wanted to explain something but he couldn't get the words out. "You might say that," he finally said. "But we must all be good to her and not cross her. Women—even the best of 'em, like Mamma—ain't like us," he went on. "When they're under the weather, they're not themselves, seems like."

"Why?"

Papa shrugged. "Only woman I ever knew wasn't like that was your own mother." He blinked a couple times and then went back to forking fresh straw into the stalls. "When your mamma says things, don't contradict, just say all right and let 'em slide right off your back. If it gets too rough, come and talk to me."

"And you won't tell her about it?"

"Not on your life!"

I felt better then, closer to Papa than I had for a long while. "You better put Genevieve wise when she comes home for her vacation," I said, "or the fur'll fly."

"I'm aimin' to have a talk with her," Papa said.

When the time came for the showers to slack off and permit the wheat to ripen, they stopped—stopped entirely. Mamma did not actually take credit for this. All she said was, "I *knew* they would." But somebody Up There, or Down Below, always seemed to swat us with something she had not anticipated and prepared for.

This year it was Hot Winds.

The grain did not ripen into full rich kernels. Instead, the sudden and prolonged hot winds dried it out and shriveled it in the pods. The spring prediction of twenty to twenty-five bushels per acre now began to shrink to fifteen or twenty, and we had better get it cut and bound while the getting was good. Hail might be out of the question to Mamma, but Papa watched every cloud that dared show its head over the Crazy Mountains.

The morning Papa and Jim were preparing the big binder for its debut performance—sharpening the sickles, fitting and tightening the canvas conveyors, checking out the binding and tying mechanisms—Fly began to deliver her colt. This was her first, and she was overdue. She moaned and groaned and snorted, and her eyes were glazed with pain, but Papa said there was nothing he could do to help her beyond making sure the colt was in the right position to make his appearance head first; which Papa did by greasing his hand and arm with tallow and reaching inside her. He could feel the little nose and the hooves of the forefeet. From here on, he said, it was just up to nature.

Nature took her own sweet time. Fly was alone in the corral and I watched her and reported every twitch to Papa and Jim during the day, once telling them she was dead because she had not moved for five minutes. But at four in the afternoon the clean little hooves and black nose appeared, and a minute later we could see that there was a star on the foal's forehead. Then suddenly it was sprawling on the ground, spider-legged, head bobbing crazily. A little stallion, Papa announced. "You oughta be shamed o' yourse'f," Jim said, "hurting your little ole mamma thataway."

Fly was too weak to get up for a while, but she whinnied to let the little fellow know she was close by, and the colt answered in a high, nervous treble. That seemed to give Fly the strength to make it to her feet. "Get away from the colt, Dale," Papa said. "You take any breed of female—she's cantankerous around her young."

Fly nuzzled the little thing and licked his face, and in a few minutes the foal tried to stand up. It was funny, but it made you want to cry, too. Papa shook his head. "A colt can do that inside o' ten minutes, and it takes a human about a year."

Genevieve timed her vacation to help with the harvest. She was good with horses and could operate the binder so long as some man was out in the field to help with repairs if anything broke down. That would leave Papa and Jim to do the rough work of shocking, which would have blistered Genevieve's hands even with gloves on.

Papa made the first cut around the field, though. Mamma came out to watch him as he lined up the binder. "Here goes nothin'!" he yelled, then clucked to the horses and cracked the whip. We all cheered as he let the unwieldy and complicated contraption into gear. It chuckled and rattled and sizzled and churned all at once. The reel turned, its blades bending the wheat onto the sickle, which sliced it off clean and flopped it onto the flat conveyor. That in turn deposited it onto the elevating apron, which lifted it into the packer. When that was full, the mechanism for which the whole machine was named took over: the binder. It bound each bundle with twine, tied it, and ejected it automatically onto the carrier.

When the carrier held three or four bundles, the driver pulled a lever that dropped them to the ground. Next time round the field, he would deposit his bundles in the stubble parallel with the first. The size of the wheat crop could be judged with some accuracy by the distance between rows. This year, though, we had better not count our chickens before they were hatched, everybody warned. The stalks looked good, but who knew for sure what was in those whiskered heads? You feared the worst but hoped for the best.

When the binder had cut its first three swaths around the field, Papa and Jim began to shock the bundles. I could carry one at a time, which was some small help, but to start a shock you needed big hands and the strength to pick up two at a time and sock them down together, butt first, so that they would stand upright and act as supports for the others to lean against in the shock.

It was late the first day, while Jim was beginning a shock, that the rattler got him.

Whether the snake had been bound up in a bundle of wheat and fell out as Jim picked it up, or merely lay hidden in the new stubble, we never knew. But suddenly, as Jim whomped his first two bundles onto the ground, he let out a yelp. I looked across the field at him and he was staring at his right forearm. Papa was running toward him from the next row where he had been building his own shocks.

By the time I got there, Papa had yanked a hunk of twine off a bundle of wheat and was drawing it tight around Jim's upper arm. He tied it, then whipped out his jackknife and examined the two small red dots where the snake had struck. "Shouldn't I kill the rattler?" Jim was asking, watching the thing slither off into the stubble.

"Hell, it's probably pizined itself biting you," Papa said, trying to make Jim laugh and stop shaking. "If it don't die, we'll take care of it later. First let's see if we can save a little souvenir here for Pocahontas."

"Her name is Fern!" Jim managed to get out between his chattering teeth before Papa could make a couple quick jabs with his knife. *"Kee-riste!"* he yelled.

"None of that talk in front of the boy," Papa said sternly, but I don't think Jim heard him. He was looking at the blood on his arm and turning pale.

"Can you suck it, or you want I should?" Papa asked.

"I kin," Jim said, and did. He'd suck a mouthful and then spit it out, suck another and spit that out.

Papa kept on talking to him, joshing him. I held my breath, wondering if at any minute Jim might keel over and stiffen out and turn black, which I had heard happened to people bitten by rattlesnakes. I remember thinking, Gee, I'm sure glad Shep's not here, he'd go for that old snake and we could never stop him. (We had had to leave Shep tied up at the house while the binder was in operation. Papa said if we didn't the damn fool was sure to wander into the sickle and get his legs cut off.)

Finally Papa asked, "How you feel, boy?"

Jim stopped sucking his arm and stared at it. You could see him trying to figure out how he felt. That's easier said than done when you're scared to death. "Okay . . . I reckon," he finally answered.

Papa untied the piece of binder twine from around Jim's upper arm and told him to hold his hand up high so the cut would stop bleeding faster.

Genevieve was coming toward us with the binder. It was near sundown anyhow, about time to call it a day, so she and Papa unhitched. Papa told Jim to get on one of the horses. He could ride home tonight like a regular grand marshal. When we got to the barn, Papa told Genevieve to take Jim on up to the house and tell Mamma to give him some of that medicine he kept for special occasions. Snakebite sure as hell better come under the head of special occasions, he said. If it got to be a regular thing, Jim could become a souse.

Naturally they told Mamma what had happened. She got the half pint of whiskey from behind the bottle of ketchup in the kitchen cabinet, and Jim drank it all down while he was scrubbing up at the washstand outside. Then while Mamma made the johnnycake, she repeated the Scientific Statement of Being several times.

Jim did not show for supper. I was worried about him because his gait on the way to the bunkhouse had been unsteady, but Papa checked on him and reported that he seemed all right. At least his heart was beating strong, his forehead felt cool, and he was snoring.

Next morning Jim was off his feed and only ate a half a dozen pancakes, but he went out to work with the rest of us. The snakebite had left him with a throbbing headache, but Papa said that was to be expected and he should take it easy for a while. Fresh air and exercise in moderation was the ticket for that kind of headache. It would probably pass entirely if he could keep his lunch down.

He could, but Jim said if it had been anything else except getting the wheat shocked before it rained or hailed, he'd sure as hell have begged off work that day.

"You sound like a Wobbly," Papa laughed. "You even smell a little like one when you stand upwind."

"SOME CHOOSE NOT TO HEAR."

Twenty-Two

Though it seemed as if Mamma and Genevieve had declared a truce, it was not as much fun to have Genevieve at home that summer. She worked so hard that she was played out at the end of the day and just flopped into bed—mine—while I bunked in the bunkhouse again with Jim. But this was no treat because Jim couldn't think about anything except why Fern hadn't answered his last letter. Genevieve had brought some new sheet music to play in case any of her old beaus stopped by, but this time of year they were all harvesting too. At the end of a long day they did not feel much like riding five or ten miles to sing "The Trail of the Lonesome Pine" and "How Would You Like to Be My Pony Girl?"

We knocked off work Sunday, though Papa wasn't sure we ought to. He would never forgive himself if it hailed when he might have saved just that much more wheat, but Mamma said she doubted very much that God would punish any man for ceasing his labors to worship Him on the Lord's day. If God could lay off from the creation of the world on the Seventh Day, then we could do no less.

Saturday night, though Genevieve was dog-tired, she decided that she would go to a dance with Manda Gullard. Every Saturday there was a shindig at the Tipperary Dance Hall out on the plains some ten miles southwest of Acton, but Manda had a fast little filly and Papa said Genevieve could ride Dan, his new saddle horse, if she thought she could handle him. Dan was a roan, rangy and mean and spirited, and Papa said he sometimes wondered if Dan wasn't locoed. He shied at rabbits and Russian thistles, and once when Papa had ridden him to Acton and a train had come through, he had run away. Papa simply let him run as long as he felt like it, and when he no longer felt like it, he whipped him and made him keep running until he yelled Uncle. Dan would never try that one again as long as Papa was riding him, but maybe he'd think he could get away with it with a girl.

Genevieve said she would take a chance. She and Manda wore their riding skirts and put their dancing duds in flour sacks tied to their saddles. When they got there two and a half hours later, it was dark enough so they hid behind their horses and changed clothes and looked fresh as paint when they pranced into the Tipperary Dance Hall.

They did not get home until nine o'clock in the morning. Genevieve wanted to go right to bed, but Mamma reminded her it was Sunday. If a person could dance all night, she said, she could stay awake for another hour to listen to the reading of this week's lesson, which Mamma had already charted out. That was one of the good things about being in Science, Mamma said. Even though you were unable to go to church, you could read the very same words that were being read there. About all you missed was the hymns.

I was Second Reader, and Mamma, First. That is, I read the texts from the Bible, and Mamma contributed Mrs. Eddy's interpretation from *Science and Health*.

While I still stumbled over some of the Biblical names and places, Mamma read with feeling, fervor, and conviction. Nevertheless, we soon lost our audience. Papa always nodded at the best of sermons, and Genevieve finally went fast asleep. I said I thought we'd better call it quits but Mamma went right on as if she hadn't noticed. When we finished, she said, "It is not our fault that some choose not to hear."

I turned eight years old while Genevieve was at home, but it was just another working Thursday for everybody. Besides, eight did not seem like much of a birthday. I had not grown more than half an inch, and I felt just the same on August 15 as I had on August 14. I would be in the fourth grade when school began next month, but what were grades anyhow when you stayed in the same room in the same school and had the same teacher? Just a new set of textbooks.

We finished the harvest Saturday and Papa and I took Genevieve to the train at Acton Sunday. It was the first time Papa had had a chance to be alone with her since she had been at home—of course I was along, but that didn't count—and while we waited for the train in the shadow of

Acton's new grain elevator he got around to asking how everything was going with her. Did she like her job, for one thing?

It was all right, she said, until she found something that paid more—or got married.

Was she thinking about getting married?

She was thinking about it. In fact, she was engaged—this made the third time but—she wasn't certain sure. It was high time she got married, she knew that. Next year she would be twenty, and that's when people began to look at you as if you were an old maid. But, she said, though she was in love with this Tom Fowler who worked in men's haberdashery at Hart-Albin's, and he wanted her to quit work and marry him, recently she had met a young fellow named Hugh Mauk from Boulder, Colorado. Hugh said he was seriously considering coming up to Billings to go into the grocery business. If he did, he hoped he could see her once in a while.

"And I feel like I want to see him," Genevieve said, wrinkling her brow. "If I was madly in love with Tom, would I be thinking about Hugh?" she asked Papa.

Papa's advice was not to tie herself down to any man until the right one blotted every other one out of the picture. A girl could be twenty-one, twenty-two, these days and still be in the running. That made Genevieve feel better in one way, but on the other hand, how was she going to break the news to Tom? The one before Tom had actually cried.

"That's the chance you've got to take," Papa said. "Better he should cry now than marry you and find you looking over the fence later."

The threshing machine could not make it up on the rim until the second week in September. Papa and Jim had been following it around the flats below us for a week or so before that, as had all the menfolk. Nobody paid anybody anything, except the owner of the threshing machine and engine. The neighbors pitched in, each with his team and hayrack, and helped each other out.

But finally came the day when the awkward mammoth, with its trunk folded over its back like an elephant spraying itself, lumbered up the road past the house and the engineer set up its first location at the far end of section 33. Papa said each setup was a tricky feat of calculating. The thresher and the steam engine that powered it had to be separated by a distance of seventy-five feet or so. Otherwise, sparks might set fire to one of the loaded hayracks and the whole shooting match would go up in smoke.

The power was carried from the flywheel of the engine to the drive wheel of the threshing machine by a huge conveyor belt slung in the form of an elongated, reclining figure eight. Consequently both machines had to be lined up within a fraction of an inch on the dead level, or the belt, traveling thirty miles an hour, could ripple and flip off its wheels and tear a man's head or arm off.

I wanted to be out there with the men but Papa said he'd have to do without me this year because Mamma needed me at the house. The neighbor women could not come to help each other; with the men gone all day, somebody had to stay home to do the chores.

Mamma and I set up planks on sawhorses in front of the house to serve as a table. The night before, Papa killed, plucked, and dressed a dozen of the chickens which I felt that I personally had hatched, and during the morning Mamma fried them and made beans and potato salad, while I sliced six loaves of bread, helped with setting the table, and baked and frosted both a white and a chocolate cake, each the size of 12-by-20 inch bread pans. Mamma promised she would never tell the men I had done it; it was humiliating enough to be eight years old and not out helping in the fields. She would merely explain that I was under the weather today.

Around twelve o'clock the threshers descended on us like a swarm of locusts, twenty-five or more riding a couple of the empty hayracks. Their hair and cheeks were streaked with sweat and dirt as they lined up to wash. Their faces were leathery and sunburned, hands calloused and cracked, bodies itchy from straw and chaff that permeated their overalls and underwear.

They were ravenous and thirsty, lusty and salty, and full of josh and brag with one another, but watchful of their language and respectful when confronted by the lady of the house, and altogether wonderful. They were doing men's work, doing it with and for one another with no reward expected, which was the way such work should be done. It was men's work, and there was not one among them who was not a man.

All conversation ceased when Mamma rang the dinner bell. They fell to at the table like prisoners not permitted to communicate with one another. Alligators could not have gulped the food faster or a pack of hounds licked the plates cleaner. What had taken all night and all morning to prepare disappeared in twenty minutes. When it was gone, they wasted no time on table talk but headed for the wheat field with renewed muscle and vigor.

I went back with them that afternoon and watched the blower build its second bright yellow strawstack. I drove Sam and old Babe as we collected a load of wheat, Jim forking the bundles up to Papa, and he distributing and stacking them so we'd have a good, solid load. Then we drove back to the roaring thresher, awaited our turn behind old Chris and Carl Gullard, and finally drew up alongside the jiggling maw of the threshing machine.

Papa and Jim forked the bundles onto the apron, which delivered them under the whirling, chattering teeth, where they exploded and were sucked inside the mysterious cavern of the machine. The straw and chaff came out of the blower like buckshot. At the side of the thresher stood the sackers, two dusty men who sacked and tied the grain as it poured out of a funnel after being cleaned by the shaking, chattering sieves inside.

Nobody talked. The roar of the thresher made that impossible. It was all you could do to make your team respond to your "Giddap" when the hayrack was finally empty.

The threshers finished up with us on the second day. We could not tell for sure how much wheat we had until we hauled it to Acton and the elevator man weighed it. But, from the look of things, Papa calculated the crop had gone about sixteen bushels to the acre. It was probably second-grade durum, so we would not get top price. The top price, meanwhile, had tumbled to sixty-five cents.

Still and all, Papa said, we had a lot to be thankful for. We had made a start this year. We could pay most of the bills, send a token to Uncle Charlie on section 33, and the bank would know our intentions were good. And the most important thing, we had our health, which, when you came right down to it, was all that counted.

"All except Mamma," I said.

"Don't worry about Mamma," Papa said. "She'll be herself again one of these days."

"I sure hope so," I said.

"CROSS YOUR HEART
AND HOPE TO DIE."

Twenty-Three

The north half of section 33 would lie fallow next year while we gave the south a chance to deliver us its bounty. Maybe next year that would be twenty-five or thirty bushels to the acre. This year it looked as if we had set our sights a little too high. If you say twenty-five or thirty instead of forty or fifty, then you won't be so let down when you don't fill all the gunnysacks you've bought. Then too, Papa said, that would give God room to maneuver and surprise you, in case He felt like dealing you a good hand.

Maybe next year . . . think about next year. Everything had to be better, unless of course the Democrats got in with that professor fellow Woodrow Wilson, and the big mucketymucks locked up their pangabooks.

Once more the sun was cooling off and throwing long thin shadows even at noontime. The storm windows were on and chinked, the potatoes and pumpkins and squash stowed away in the darkness of the root cellar. I found three moss agates and two Indian arrowheads—what had they been aimed at? a wolf? an elk? a white man?—and Jim shot a deer while we were cutting firewood on the rim. We had fresh venison for a few days, gave some to our neighbors, and Mamma made mincemeat out of the rest. Aunt Edie and Uncle Corve were coming over for Thanksgiving dinner, and we could have mince pies as well as pumpkin, though Mamma did not seem in any condition to cook a big dinner. She was tired all the time. She would get up in the morning tired and go to bed tired, even when there was not much to do.

School soon settled into its routine, except for one thing. We had a new pupil just about my age. Niles Newcomb, who had proved up on his homestead, had gone back East and brought home a new wife. She had been a widow with a son named Oscar. They not only lived within a mile of us, but Oscar had a priceless quality as the playmate of a small boy like me: he was even smaller. I must have towered a good two inches over him and had five pounds on him. It made me feel superior to look down on another kid, just as living up on the rim made us superior to those down in the gumbo flats.

I had been walking to school because Fly had to stay home to nurse her colt. But early in November Papa said it was time to start weaning the colt, so I strapped the surcingle on Fly and rode her. I caught up with Selma Gullard, who was still walking, and she crawled up behind me.

Selma got to talking about how she was learning to cook; Manda was teaching her, and she could already make a johnnycake. But she wondered if Mamma would tell her how to make that devil's food cake that she served to the threshers? Her brother Carl had been talking about it ever since. He said it was the best thing he ever put into his mouth.

That was too much for me. I said I would tell her a secret if she crossed her heart and hoped to die before she repeated it. Naturally she crossed her heart and hoped to die, and I told her that it wasn't Mamma, it was me who had baked the cake.

Selma was still calling me a liar when we arrived at the schoolhouse and she told not only Miss Moody but Oscar Newcomb. I reminded her that she had crossed her heart and hoped to die, but she said crossing your heart and hoping to die could be King's-exed when you'd promised a liar. I finally threw caution to the winds and told her she could ask Mamma if she did not believe me.

Miss Moody stood up for me halfheartedly. She said that she had never heard tell of a boy of eight learning to cook, but it was no disgrace so far as she knew. But Oscar thought it was and said so out back of the horse shed at recess. His mother wouldn't let him cook, even if he wanted to help her out, which he didn't. Once he had asked her to teach him how to make oatmeal, and she wouldn't. She said a boy could build a fire and set the teakettle on, but from there on he'd better skidoo because it was sissy for a boy to cook.

I said, "What about Peterson? He cooks. You better not let him hear you calling him a sissy."

And Oscar said, "He's an old bach. They're different."

"Are you calling me a sissy?" I yelled.

"Yeah. I'm callin' you a sissy," he said and stuck out his chin.

So I hit it and knocked him down. I had been knocked down and sat on by bigger boys in Neillsville any number of times, but I had never knocked anybody down before (or since, I may say). Now there Oscar lay, flat on the ground, with a trickle of blood oozing out of his mouth, looking up at me as if he was scared. Somebody scared of me? Well. I'd make him good and scared.

I jumped on him and started pounding him in the ribs, saying, "Take that back, you little shrimp," and yelling so loud I couldn't hear him saying Uncle.

Then Miss Moody was there and lifted me off by the scruff of the neck and told me I was a bully and should be ashamed of myself. But I wasn't. I had never in my wildest fantasies dared hope to be called a bully. I felt ten feet tall that whole day, and glared at Oscar every chance I got, to try to make him look scared again.

I could not wait to get home and tell Jim about my triumph. Unfortunately, neither could Fly wait to get home to her colt. She took off on a dead run before Selma could even climb up behind me. I grabbed the surcingle and held on but when she started down the slope of the big ravine that transected section 29 I began to slide forward and there was no more holding on. I hoped for the best until I looked down and saw Fly's ears disappearing between my legs, and then felt the thump of the ground and the excruciating jab of cactus needles.

I was jarred up pretty thoroughly, but it is no fun to sit in a cactus bed so I got out as fast as I could. Fly had stopped dead when I slipped over her head but I did not even try to get on her back again. I let her go and walked on home, bawling my head off.

Papa laid me prone on the kitchen table, took my pants down, said I looked as if I'd backed into a porkypine, and decided pliers were the only solution. One by one he yanked the cactus needles out, and Mamma painted the bloody scars with iodine. When they were finished, Papa took a last look. If things got really tough, he said, trying to make me laugh, he could hire me out as a baboon with Ringling Brothers Circus. That did not seem funny at the time.

As if to compound the pain and the indignity, Mamma broke the news that Jim would be leaving us soon—not merely for the winter this time, but for keeps. He had had a letter from Fern telling him that while she was still very fond of him and hoped he would always remain her friend, she had fallen in love with her mother's second cousin—funny, I had never thought of Indians as having cousins or uncles and aunts—and had decided to marry him. He was a full-blooded Crow, and she thought marriage with him would stand a better chance, not so much because they were both Indians but because they were both Roman Catholic converts.

"The girl sounds like she's got a head on her shoulders," Papa commented.

So Jim, after two years with us, would soon be resuming his restless odyssey to take a gander at the other side of the Rocky Mountains and squint into a sunset over the Pacific Ocean. He would be leaving around Thanksgiving time. We could get along without a hired man till spring.

Something woke me up in the middle of the night. I thought at first Mamma had another one of her sick headaches—she had not had one since last spring—and was moaning. But it was only the November north wind tuning up for winter, so I snuggled down and tried to put myself back to sleep.

Mamma said that since she had been in Science, thinking beautiful thoughts often put her to sleep. Now, what was a beautiful thought? Well, Uncle Corve and Aunt Edie were coming over for Thanksgiving dinner tomorrow and bringing the turkey. They had experimented this year with a setting of white turkey eggs and while some of the stupid birds had wandered off and been killed by coyotes, they had managed to raise half a dozen. Aunt Edie had written that she would stuff and cook the bird the night before and then we would only have to warm it up after they got here.

That was a beautiful thought, but I was still wide awake and, much as I tried, I could not help thinking about Jim, who was going as far as Acton with Aunt Edie and Uncle Corve when they went home. Papa had settled up with him for his eight months' work, even paying him for the full month of November. He had $240 and was rich.

Jim was going to catch the train north tomorrow afternoon. He said he might as well take a look-see at Great Falls and Butte while he was in Montana. He might never pass this way again.

That was not a beautiful thought.

Papa and Mamma were both worried about Jim carrying all that money on him and warned him not to let strangers know he had it. You heard stories about the slickers around Butte and Anaconda. Maybe Jim ought to collect only part of what was owed him and write us when he needed more of it. How would that be?

Jim said he had learned his lesson. He had been drugged and rolled once back there in Deadwood, and once burned, twice shy, even when a nice lady asks you to go upstairs and listen to her graphophone.

But maybe, I thought, maybe he hadn't learned his lesson all that good, or if he had, maybe some slicker would try a slicker trick on him. Then Jim would have to come back to us next year. That was not a beautiful thought so far as Jim was concerned, but it put me to sleep.

"SHAKE HANDS
WITH BACON."

Twenty-Four

By morning the wind had wearied of its wailing and groaning and settled down to business—a steady sixty-mile-an-hour gale out of the west. There was some conjecture about whether Uncle Corve and Aunt Edie could make it on a day like this, but Papa said he was betting on Corve. They would have no trouble driving from their place to ours—the wind would practically blow them. Going back would be a horse of another color, but well hell, Corve was a sport, Papa said. He'd take a chance on the wind letting up by late afternoon.

After the chores and breakfast, and while Mamma prepared the pies for the oven, Jim heated a boiler of water on the cookstove and Papa helped him lug it to the bunkhouse to take a bath. Lord only knew, he said, when he might have a chance to take another. After his bath he even shaved and put on his suit, and I helped him pack his grip.

"What are you going to do about your bearskin?" I asked him.

That had been bothering him a heap, he said. He had thought about leaving it with us. He still would, if Mamma had her heart set on it, but it meant a lot to him and if Mamma didn't particularly want it, why, he thought he'd take it along with him.

I told him that Mamma still had no place for it so it would have to be left out here in the bunkhouse anyhow, and probably our hired man next year wouldn't appreciate it.

He had thought about that too, Jim said, and he didn't cotton to the notion of some other hired man warming his dirty feet on it. "You better take it along," I said, but I didn't wait to watch him stuff it in a gunnysack. I was afraid I might start to sniffle. Anyhow, Shep had been limping and had told me he'd stepped on a cactus. I had to see if I could get the needle out.

At about eleven o'clock Mamma sent me to the root cellar to fetch her a jar of green tomato pickles. Fighting my way back to the house against the gale, I happened to glance off down the road and saw an automobile coming. It was kicking up a cloud of dust that flattened out ahead of it a good half mile. I could tell by the brass headlamps that it was a Tin Lizzie. A man was driving it and a woman sat beside him. It was not until they stopped for the woman to get out and open the gate down past the barn that I realized who it was: Aunt Edie and Uncle Corve!

I forgot all about the green tomato pickles and ran to meet them. Uncle Corve had maneuvered the car through the gate by then and Aunt Edie was closing it. "My hat!" she screamed. The wind had blown her hat off, and it was cartwheeling up the rise. I finally caught up with it and brought it back.

By that time Uncle Corve had the automobile braked to a stop in the shelter of the house, but he didn't dare get out and let up on the brake—the emergency, he yelled, might not hold her still against the wind—until Papa, who had come out to look into the cause of the racket, had found a couple blocks of wood to jam behind the wheels.

Then Uncle Corve got out, and the three of us—Papa, Jim, and me—stood there admiring it, while Shep came up, gave one of the wheels a sniff, and then baptized it.

"I'll be damned, Corve!" Papa said. "I got to hand it to you!"

"Yeah?" Uncle Corve said, pleased. "Well, it's probably a damn-fool thing to do, but it kinda took my eye."

"You *did* it!" I yelled, remembering back to last April, when the two of us walked into the agency together.

"You never spilled," he said, poking me in the ribs.

"Not me!"

"The kid knew all along I might give in and do it," Uncle Corve explained.

"What did Aunt Edie have to say?" I wanted to know.

"Go ask her," Uncle Corve said. From the way he said it, though, I knew that Aunt Edie had come around.

Uncle Corve opened up a drawer behind the seat and lifted out the turkey, which was wrapped in oiled paper and tied with twine. Then the four of us crowded into the house.

"Shut that door!" Mamma cried, as if she were mad.

Aunt Edie and Uncle Corve exchanged glances while he handed her the turkey. "How're you, Jessie?" he said.

"I'm fine," she said. Her face was flushed from the heat of the stove or something.

"Anything wrong?" Uncle Corve asked.

"Not a thing. Not with *me*."

"That's the spirit," Uncle Corve said. "Happy Thanksgiving to you."

"It must be a *very* happy Thanksgiving for some, Corve. I didn't know your crop was so much better than ours."

"Now what do you mean by that, Jess?" I guess he had missed the warning look from Aunt Edie.

"What I mean is, *some* don't scatter their money to the four winds just to put on the dog."

A remark like that would have made a lot of people boiling mad, but not Uncle Corve. He just went up to Mamma and hugged her and said, "Let the steam out o' your boiler, Jessie. Edie and me, we don't have so much time left to enjoy these newfangled things. And we got nobody to leave all our millions to, like you and Bob, so . . ."

"Mamma's glad you got a Tin Lizzie if you want it," Papa said. "I'll buy her one myself one of these days, when our ship comes in."

Mamma was still staring down at the stove, but she was not saying anything, so it probably would not be long before she changed the subject. Uncle Corve took his watch out of his pocket and opened it. "Just one hour ago," he said, "we was ten miles from here, and we already been here fifteen minutes. Seems hard to believe, don't it?

Why, when we get the turnpike graded, we'll be less'n half an hour apart."

There was a knock on the door. It was Harry and Carl Gullard. They'd seen the Tin Lizzie coming up the road past the Newcombs and wanted to have a look at it. We left Mamma and Aunt Edie inside and went out to show it off. Uncle Corve said there was just one thing bothered him. When he cranked the engine, it sometimes kicked the daylights out of him.

Harry, who knew all about gasoline engines, had some good advice. He said when Uncle Corve cranked the engine to have Aunt Edie sit behind the steering wheel with the spark lever way up. As soon as the engine caught and began to turn over, then she could pull down on the spark for more power. If you cranked with the spark down, though, you could break your arm.

When we went inside again the clouds had lifted. Mamma was joking and even went so far as to say that one of these days—not just yet awhile, but one of these days—she would let Uncle Corve take her for a ride. "Atsa stuff," Uncle Corve chuckled.

But later that day Mamma did have the last laugh.

The wind kept on howling. Every once in a while Uncle Corve would glance out the window to make sure the Tin Lizzie was not taking off over the rim along with the tumbleweeds. But inside the house it was cozy and warm, and after we were stuffed with turkey and rolls and pie and all the fixings, Mamma asked me to tell the story of the Pilgrims' first Thanksgiving. We had just studied that at school.

Uncle Corve folded his hands over his paunch, leaned back, smiled, and belched. "There goes Vesuvius," Aunt

Edie said, right on cue. Uncle Corve said, "Excuse me," and closed his eyes. He claimed he could listen better with his eyes closed. That way nothing would distract him. When he began to snore gently, Aunt Edie poked him and made him wake up.

While Mamma and Aunt Edie washed the dishes, the menfolk talked about the world events, like what was Pancho Villa up to these days, and that pesky war in the Balkans. Danged if it didn't seem like there was always a war in the Balkans, wherever they were, Uncle Corve opined. "I never was very good at geography," he said.

Mamma said that the Balkans were somewhere between Switzerland and Turkey. They were countries like Romania and Montenegro, but for some reason not Greece. Gypsies and trash like that came from around there. She had read a book about the Balkans not long ago: *The Prisoner of Zenda.* Of course the hero of that was uppercrust, not a gypsy.

Well, no matter, Uncle Corve said. Or did it? Were those wars way off there at the root of prices going up?—all except the prices of farmers' produce, that is.

Probably not, Papa said. You could lay that on the doorstep of the Democrats. A party that would elect a college professor President couldn't be trusted. We were in for hard times sure as God made little green apples, but maybe if the country got enough of him and repudiated Wilson next time around, we could avoid another panic like 1907.

By two o'clock Uncle Corve began to fuss and fume. He wanted to be sure he could make it home before dark; in a wind like this he'd hate to try to light the headlamps—not that they did much good, even when they were lit. Some one of those geniuses back there working for Henry Ford should do something about the headlamp before they brought out the next Model T.

Papa said, "Set a spell, Corve. The sun don't go down till around four-fifteen. You said yourself you made it over here in less'n an hour."

"That was with the wind behind us," Uncle Corve said. "And we got more to carry going home." He patted his stomach.

Aunt Edie laughed. It wasn't so much that Corve wanted to get home early, she said, he just couldn't keep his hands off that blame car. Why, he was as excited about it as he had been when he first got a job as motorman in Coeur d'Alene. There was something about a machine that turned a grown man into an eight-year-old.

But about three, Uncle Corve said, "No kidding, Edie, get bundled up. We got to get started." Then he turned to Jim. "Understand you want a lift to Acton."

"That's about the size of it, Mr. Ransimer, if you got room."

"We can make room," Aunt Edie said.

While Jim went to the bunkhouse to collect his gear and put on his cap and sheepskin coat, Papa and I took Uncle Corve to the barn to have a look at Fly's colt, Randy, who was almost four months old by now. Randy was gentle like his mother. I showed Uncle Corve how he would come to you when you called him by name—of course you had to offer him a carrot at first to train him. While I was feeding him the carrot, Uncle Corve said, "Next thing you know, you'll be reading books to the colt, too, eh?"

"No," I said, "he's just a horse."

Uncle Corve looked at Papa. "Meaning horses ain't as smart as dogs, is that it?"

I pretended not to hear that, and then Papa said, "Answer your Uncle Corve, Dale. He asked you a question."

"I guess not," I said.

"Remember what we were talking about over to your place sometime ago?" Papa said. Uncle Corve nodded. "Well, I wish you'd tell him what you said to me."

Papa walked out of the barn and left me alone with Uncle Corve. He picked up a straw and began to chew on it. Then he asked me if I still claimed I could understand what Shep was thinking. When I didn't answer, he said to tell him the truth; he wouldn't tell Mamma.

So I told him the truth. Yes, I could—not all the time, but most of the time.

Uncle Corve sucked on his straw and frowned. "You don't look like you're lying," he said, "but of course you are. Unless you're tetched. I got to admit I been worrying about you ever since I seen you reading that book to that fool dog."

"He's not a fool dog!" I said. "He's my friend."

"Keep your shirt on," Uncle Corve said. "A dog can be a good friend to a boy. But you can't talk to one another."

"I can," I said. "And Shep can."

Uncle Corve gave me a long look and then he told me about a little boy he had known way back there in the seventies. This little boy had been an only child and lived on a farm outside of West Bend, and his name was Willis. "I'll never forget him—nice-looking kid, red-headed," Uncle Corve said. Well, this little boy was now locked up in a loony bin in Wisconsin somewhere. Had been for years and years. And it had all begun when Willis began to imagine he had a playmate called Bacon. "That dang kid would walk up to you and say, 'Shake hands with Bacon,' and if you didn't shake hands with nothing, because of course it wasn't nothing, there wasn't any kid named Bacon, why Willis would yell and kick you in the shins. His folks didn't know what to do about him. Worried sick, they were. They used to whip him and try to get him to admit there wasn't no such a thing as Bacon, but it didn't do no good." Uncle Corve gave his head a rueful shake. "Finally had to put the kid away."

Well, you couldn't blame Willis's folks for that, I told Uncle Corve. What else could they do? Making up a kid to play with, why, that was loony. The loony bin was where he belonged.

Uncle Corve shrugged his shoulders. He had tried, hadn't he? Then we joined Papa, who was waiting outside. Uncle Corve shook his head. "If I was in your shoes, Bob," he said, "I'd sure as hell separate 'em."

Finally they were ready to start. Aunt Edie, her hat tied firmly under her chin, sat under the wheel with the spark lever way up and the gas halfway down. Uncle Corve gave the crank a couple whirls and the motor caught. Aunt Edie yanked down on both spark and gas and the thing roared and spat and then settled down.

Jim had lashed his grip and the gunnysack containing his bearskin over the drawer at the back. There wasn't enough room for him inside, but it was only four miles to Acton and he could stand on the running board that far.

As Aunt Edie slid over to the right, Uncle Corve climbed into the driver's seat. He grinned and said he had a little trouble getting all that turkey under the steering wheel. Jim shook hands with Mamma and Papa and I could see Mamma saying "Write to us, Jim," but of course her voice could not be heard over the wind and the roaring and rattling of the Tin Lizzie. Jim came up to me and said, "So long." We shook hands, and then I went inside the house because I didn't want anybody to see me clouding up just because Jim was leaving.

I looked out at them from behind the lace curtain at the window. Jim was standing on the running board and Uncle Corve was gripping the wheel. He was giving the Tin Lizzie all the gas there was in her and he was jamming down on low till a vein bulged out on his forehead. And Henry Ford's monument was not budging an inch. In fact, when Uncle Corve finally let up on low, she started to back up because her top ballooned like a sailboat's spinnaker. If Uncle Corve hadn't grabbed the emergency she would probably have backed right on up the rise and disappeared.

I went back outside. Mamma was laughing fit to kill and slapping her sides. "Corve," she gasped and cried, "get a horse."

Uncle Corve could not hear her but he could see her face and so could Aunt Edie. "Don't worry," Aunt Edie snapped, "we'll make it!"

"I'll get off and push," Jim said. He did, and nothing happened. "Clutch seems to be slipping," Uncle Corve yelled.

Then Papa had an idea. If Uncle Corve would back the Tin Lizzie to the top of the rise and then give her all she had in her, plus gravity, they might get her going into the wind. Anyhow, it was worth a try.

Uncle Corve let up on the brake, jammed down on the middle reverse pedal, and started to back her up the rise. He hit a gopher hole, and the sack containing Jim's bearskin fell off and the Tin Lizzie backed right over it. Jim picked it up, but the gunnysack had split and spilled the pelt out. Aunt Edie reached for it and plopped it on her lap. Meanwhile I hurried down to the gate by the barn, so once underway, the car wouldn't have to come to another stop while somebody opened the gate.

I finally got it open. Papa and Jim got behind the Tin Lizzie and gave her a shove. She bucked forward and Jim trotted alongside, then leapt on the fender. They ran smack into a tumbleweed that got caught in the crank and almost concealed the occupants in the front seat, but they didn't dare stop to dig the thing out. They must have been hitting fifteen miles an hour—in high—by the time they sailed through the gate. Uncle Corve was grinning—and so was the bear—at Aunt Edie clutching her hat.

Jim looked back and waved at Shep and me. After a minute or so, I shut the gate. Papa was going straight across the field toward the house. Shep and I walked toward the barn. He looked up at me. He was wondering if Jim would ever come back our way. I told him I hated to admit it, but probably not. So from now on it was just him and me—Shep and me, that is.

That night I heard Mamma and Papa through the partition after they had gone to bed. Mamma was talking about Uncle Corve and the Tin Lizzie and how, much as she hated to admit it, she blamed Aunt Edie for part of it. "Edie," she said, "has always let Corve have his say about practically anything."

"Maybe she loves him," Papa said.

"All the more reason to put her foot down. You know what they say about a fool and his money."

Papa was quiet for a minute, and then he said, "The way I look at it, Jessie, when a man Corve's age gets the wants, he should get what he wants while the wanting's good."

Then Mamma was quiet. Finally she said, and her voice sounded different, "What do you want?"

"You know what I want," Papa said.

"You care what brand you get?"

"Hell, no," Papa said, "just as long as it's alive and kicking."

I heard them laughing, and then I went to sleep. Thanksgiving was over.

"TELL HIM MY
TIME HAS COME."

Twenty-Five

Papa was going to Billings on Monday, the fourteenth of December. Mamma said she didn't feel up to the trip, but Papa might run into Santa Claus at Hart-Albin's, where he sometimes put in an appearance, and I'd better make a list of things I wanted.

I had begun to suspect, the year before, that Santa Claus was your father—how could a big, fat man in all those clothes squeeze down our narrow stovepipe?—but Papa and Mamma seemed to want me to believe, so I dutifully made the list: a pair of hair clippers that wouldn't pull so; a new pencil box; a Meccano set—you could build bridges, towers, wagons, cannons, anything, with Meccano, which for some reason seemed to me infinitely superior to its carbon copy the Erector set; a Flexible Flyer; a belt with my initial on it.

Papa glanced over the list and told me not to get my hopes up—Santa Claus might be fresh out of some of those items—but he would do what he could.

Sunday afternoon, while I was practicing Mozart's "Turkish March," Niles Newcomb came by. After he had paid his respects to Mamma he asked where Papa was. "He's down to the barn oiling the harnesses," Mamma told him. Why? Was there anything special?

"Nothing to speak of," Mr. Newcomb said, but whatever it was, he and Papa spoke of it for quite a while. When Papa finally came up to the house he and Mamma went into the bedroom and talked very low. Then Papa came out and said he thought he'd take Shep to Billings with him in the morning and let a vet look him over. A coyote had died down around Buffalo Spring a short time ago and Niles said it might have been rabies killed it. "If there's rabies going around among coyotes, you should let a vet examine your dog, Niles says," Papa explained.

"But what if Shep's got rabies?" I said, swallowing hard.

Papa didn't look at me but turned to Mamma.

"We cross one bridge at a time," she said.

"If he's got 'em, it wouldn't hurt if you telephoned Mrs. Schultz and asked her to give him a treatment," I said.

Papa did not answer that. Mamma handed him the milk pail and he went down to the barn.

Monday morning was cold and still and gray. I started off for school before Papa left with Shep. He wanted to go with me as he usually did, but I explained that he had to go see the vet. "You'll be home tonight," I told him.

"Tell Him My Time Has Come."

"No, he won't," Mamma said. "Papa's not coming back till tomorrow."

"I could make it by tonight," Papa said, "if you feel uneasy."

"Nothing to feel uneasy about," Mamma said. "We'll let everything but milking slide this evening."

There were three of us at school that day—Selma, Oscar, and me. And Kate Moody. Edna Moody had the grippe and her sister was substituting. That was always fun, because Kate didn't know where we were in our lessons and she would swallow anything we told her. And if it had been Miss Edna Moody, we probably would have stayed in the schoolhouse and shivered all day.

In midmorning Peterson came by to offer to carry in wood. He saw us all sitting there with our coats and caps and mittens on and invited us over to his dugout. Kate jumped at the chance. Peterson was going hunting, he said, but he had left a fire going, and we would have the place to ourselves.

That day was not like school at all. It was warm and dark and smoky inside the dugout, and it smelled the way a saloon smells when you walk past it. There was nothing to sit on but one chair and Peterson's rumpled bed. Kate Moody took the chair and the three of us kids sat on the bed. Peterson had forgot to tell us he kept his sourdough pancake starter under the bed covers to keep it from freezing if he happened to be caught out overnight. We upset it. Miss Edna Moody would have hit the ceiling, but not Kate. She just rinsed out the blanket and hung it up to dry—inside, of course. If she had put it out on the line in December, it would have frozen solid in five minutes. Then she wrote a note telling Peterson what had happened. She said she would fetch him a new batch of starter from home tomorrow.

Along about three o'clock Kate looked out the door and told us she was going to let us out a little early. "There're sure enough two sun-dogs around the sun, and that can mean a blizzard. You dumb kids could get lost and freeze to death and they'd say it was my fault," she said. Then she grinned. "Besides, I've got a fella coming to see me tonight, and I've got to get prettied up." You couldn't help liking Kate Moody. She was full of the old Harry.

Selma and Oscar and I started out together. After a quarter of a mile Oscar would turn off to the right alone, but we always had unfinished business to talk about and stood and jabbered for five minutes before we said "So long." Today Selma finally said if I wanted to walk the rest of the way with her I'd better shake a leg because she was going on, no matter what. We were almost out of calling distance when Oscar yelled, "Did you get rid of your chicken eater?"

I didn't know what he meant. "What chicken eater?" I called.

"You know. Shep. He killed a couple of our chickens yesterday."

"You're a liar!"

"Ask Pa!" Oscar called Niles Newcomb Pa, even if he wasn't his father, the way I called Mamma, Mamma.

"I'll just do that little thing!" I said, and started off again.

"Did your father shoot him like he said he would?" he yelled.

I stopped and looked back at Oscar again. "What did you say?"

"Did your dad shoot him?"

"He wouldn't shoot Shep!" I said, and began to walk back toward Oscar.

"Then where is he today?"

"He's gone to Billings with Papa . . . to the vets, because maybe a coyote with rabies bit him!"

"Yeah. Like fun a coyote with rabies bit him. Anybody believes that's a rotten egg!"

By that time I had caught up with Oscar. "Your father told my father there was a coyote with rabies!" I told him.

"My father told your father no such of a thing," Oscar said. "Listen, if there was coyotes with rabies around here, do you think they'd let you walk to school? They'd make you ride on Fly."

I had nothing to say to that, and Oscar bored in. "Yeah-yeah, guess you didn't think of that, did you, you bully!"

No. I hadn't thought of that. I turned and started for home once more. Selma had walked on ahead, but I didn't even notice. I didn't notice her or the cold or the sun-dogs that had doubled to four or the pain that stabbed me in the chest every time I gasped for breath, until I walked into the house and screamed, "What did you do to Shep?"

Mamma was standing in front of the kitchen cabinet, rolling out a batch of oatmeal cookies. When she turned to me she pushed her hair from her forehead with the back of her right hand. It was covered with flour and streaked her hair with gray. She didn't answer but looked down at the rolling pin in her left hand. "I hate to make oatmeal cookies," she said absently. "The dough sticks like sixty."

"Did you shoot him?" I yelled.

Mamma shook her head. "Of course we didn't shoot him," she said. "Where did you get such an idea?"

"Oscar," I said. "Oscar said Shep killed their chickens and Papa promised to shoot him."

She looked around and laid the rolling pin beside the cookie dough, then she wiped her hands and sat down in the rocker. "Come here, Dale," she said. I stood my ground. "Please?" she went on.

"If he's gone for good, just say it! Say he'll never come back!"

"You're old enough to understand things now," she said. "We could put up with Shep as long as he just killed our chickens, but when he goes to the neighbors . . ."

"You lied to me!" I screamed. I looked at Mamma and I hated her, and she was red, everything was red. I grabbed the red rolling pin and tried to hit her with it, and when she wrenched that out of my hands I kicked and bit and screamed. She tried to catch me, but I picked up the egg pail and tore out of the house. I ran to the chicken coop and started gathering the eggs—I didn't know what I was doing—and when I broke one of the red eggs I began to throw the rest of them. The red chickens squawked, and their red feathers flew. Then suddenly Mamma was standing in the doorway, and I threw an egg at her and it broke, and its red yolk dribbled down her dress.

"Don't you dare do that to your mother!" she cried.

"*You're not my mother!*"

I caught my breath then. I hadn't said that. I couldn't have said that, but from the look on Mamma's red face I must have. And slowly, as she wilted against the doorjamb, she turned back to white—her face, her eyes, her hair, her dress, everything. And then the next thing I knew I was lying on the cot in the house, and Mamma was sitting beside me, smiling down at me.

"Do you want a cookie?" she said. "They're fresh out of the oven."

I shook my head. They had taken Shep away from me, and she was offering me a cookie! I tried to say "Where is he?" but I vomited instead, and Mamma had to clean up the cot.

Then she said she didn't want me to talk. She would do the talking and I was to listen. Papa had only kept Shep because I was so attached to him. Shep was no earthly use around a farm. When he had killed the guinea—and later the rooster—she and Papa had talked about giving him away and getting another dog, but they had kept him on account of me. They had talked long into the nights about what to do, especially after I had begun to claim that we talked to each other. Uncle Corve thought that was not healthy, but Mamma had hoped and prayed. Maybe I would outgrow it when I had other children to play with. Anyhow, they had put up with Shep, fenced in the chickens, and waited to see what happened.

But now that Shep had begun to kill the neighbors' chickens—well, she and Papa had no choice. She was sorry they had lied to me about taking him to the vet, but that was Papa's idea, because he didn't want to leave Mamma alone with me after I'd had a shock like that. He had planned to tell me the truth when he came home. But now it was out—no thanks to Oscar!—and she was sorry, but we had to face things like the loss of a dog—or a loved one—in this life. And I could rest easy about Shep's being well taken care of. Papa was going to see that he found a good home with some nice people in Billings who did not keep chickens.

He was going to bring home another dog tomorrow, too. He might even find a beautiful white collie like the one I had wanted to win selling subscriptions to the *Saturday Evening Post*. Wouldn't that be nice?

I didn't answer.

"Let's think about a name," she said.

I thought about a name. *Shep.* And I turned my face to the wall and thought about what I was going to do tomorrow. Long before Papa got home, I would run away—all the way to Billings—and find him and stay there with the nice people in the good home where Shep lived.

It began to snow before dark. Mamma did the milking by lantern light. She slipped and fell on the way up to the house and spilled all the milk, but she was glad I had been carrying the lantern. There would be more milk in the morning, but we had only one lantern.

After supper she was restless and sighed deep, breathcatching sighs. She tried to talk to me but I would not answer. When she asked if I would read the lesson with her, I just shook my head. This week's lesson was titled "Love," and what it said was that God was Love and Love was Good and Good was God and God was All in All, and I didn't believe it any longer. If God was All in All, how come He could do this to Shep and me?

She took the Bible and *Science and Health* into the bedroom with her and studied the lesson alone.

I don't know how long I had been asleep when I opened my eyes. Mamma had put out the lamp in the bedroom and there was no light anywhere. The wind was howling under the eaves and driving sleet and snow like buckshot against the windowpane over my cot. My nose was cold and wet. I put my hand outside the blankets and felt the snow that had sifted through a crack in the windowsill where the chinking had worked loose.

I listened to the wind and tried not to think about anything else. As long as you concentrate hard on one thing, Jim had once told me, you can't think about another. Say you're going to have to take a dose of castor oil, he said. Well, don't think about castor oil. Think about ice cream.

That did not work tonight. Thinking about what Jim said made me wonder about Jim. Where was he? Did Jim remember us and ever think about us? Where was his bearskin? And thinking about his bearskin, I suddenly saw Shep resting his head on the bear's head and looking up at us out of his watch-eye while Jim told us about the time he won—and lost—a thousand dollars at poker in Omaha, Nebraska. Jim could sure tell 'em!

There was a change in the pitch of the wind, and something else, too. It sounded like a moan. After a minute a match flickered in the bedroom. That was followed by the yellow, steady glow of lamplight. Mamma must have had a bad dream. She sometimes did when Papa was away. Then the glow in the door grew brighter.

I shut my eyes and pretended to be asleep because I still didn't want to talk to her. The next thing I knew she had set the lamp on the table and was shaking me. I opened my eyes and looked up. Mamma was wearing her old flowered flannel bathrobe. The rope around it had only one tassel—Shep had chewed the other off—and her face was shiny with sweat. She looked scared, and suddenly I felt sorry for her. Oh, I was still mad at her, and Papa too, but I couldn't help feeling sorry as well.

"Did you have a bad dream?" I asked.

"What? . . . Oh, no . . . not a bad dream," she muttered, and then she pulled up a chair and sat down beside the cot and asked me if I would be afraid to go up to the Gullards' house.

When, I wanted to know?

"Now. Tonight," she said. "Right away. I've got to get word to your father."

Word to Papa? About what?

She said she was going to be sick, awfully sick, and she had promised Papa that when her time came—and she wasn't expecting it so soon—but when her time came, no matter when it was or where he was she would tell him so he could bring a doctor.

I was sitting up by now and putting on my clothes. "But don't you want him to call Mrs. Schultz?" I said between chattering teeth. "She could give you an absent treatment."

"He'll do that too," she said. "Robert promised me that, but . . ." She stopped talking and bit her lower lip and grabbed onto the edge of the cot. Then after about half a minute she got to her feet and shook up the grate under the still-glowing coals in the pot-bellied stove and threw more wood into it. While I put on shoes and overshoes and leggings she filled the lantern with kerosene and lit the wick.

"Be careful how you carry the lantern," she said. "Keep it right side up."

"I will," I said.

"And don't you drop it or set it down, except to go through the gate." She sounded cross.

"I guess I know how to carry a lantern," I grumbled.

"Oh, I know you do," she said. "I know that." It

sounded as if she was about to cry. She grabbed me and hugged me and then pulled back and looked down at me. "You're scared!" she said. "You're shaking."

"I'm shaking, but I'm not scared," I said. "It's all these old cold clothes. I got a chill."

"I can't let you do it," she said. "I just can't let you do it."

I was buttoning my mackinaw and having trouble finding the sheepskin mittens that were sewed to a twine running up one sleeve, across the back, and down the other. One mitten always seemed to be stuck up a sleeve somewhere.

"If Shep was here he'd go with me," I mumbled.

Mamma caught her breath in a kind of a sob. "You don't need to remind me of that," she said. "That's all I've been thinking about for the last hour."

Then she stooped over, tied my old woolen muffler around my throat, gave my stocking cap a rough jerk down over the ears, and buttoned my mackinaw the way it should be. "If you hear anything," she said, "it's probably just the wind. Nothing's going to come near you as long as you keep moving and swing the lantern."

"What could come near me?" I wanted to know. I hadn't thought of anything coming near me until that moment.

"Nothing," Mamma said. "Nothing at all. Now when you get there, tell them Papa is at the Commercial Hotel tonight. Old Chris will probably send Harry or Carl to Robinson's store to telephone. Whoever goes that far might as well do us a favor and ride on over to Aunt Edie's and Uncle Corve's. I promised Edie to let her know, too."

"To let her know what, Mamma?"

"That . . . well . . ." she looked down at me and tried to

smile. "That my time has come. Just say that. The Gullards will understand."

She kissed me, and I stared at her and tried to understand what she was saying. Then she handed me the lantern and went to the door. She put her hand on the doorknob, but she did not open it for a minute. She was praying, really praying, and not just the Scientific Statement of Being either, but talking right straight to Him, saying Please God, help me, and things like that.

Then she opened the door into the woodshed and Shep was lying there on the doormat where he always lay at night. He looked just the same, except he was wearing a new collar and there was a piece of rope tied to it, and the rope was gnawed and stringy like the rope on Mamma's bathrobe.

Shep stood up and shook the snow off his back. I looked up at Mamma, who was having trouble getting her breath. "I guess he didn't like the nice people Papa gave him to, so he came home," I said. Shep wagged his tail, which of course meant that was what had happened.

Mamma bent over and stroked his head. "I thought you were a ghost," she whispered.

"He ain't no ghost," I said. "He's ole Shep." Then she kissed me and said, "If you miss the gate, just follow the fence until you come to it," and told Shep, "You take care of him, Shep."

"We're not ascared now," I said, and I wasn't, and of course Shep wasn't. If he could come twenty miles from Billings all alone into the blizzard, I guess walking another mile with me and the lantern and the wind behind us would be a cinch.

"ALL AT ONCE
I KNEW WHAT A
WATCH-EYE MEANT."

Twenty-Six

We started out. The snow was deep where it drifted around the southeast corner of the house, but other places it was only about six inches. I kept one hand on Shep's back and he stayed right beside me. When the lantern got heavy and I had to shift it to the other hand, he trotted around so that the light wouldn't separate us.

The lantern lit up the outline of the pump off to the right, where it should be, and we hurried on, following what looked like the vague, snow-covered rut of the old buffalo trail that ran from Buffalo Spring past our place and then just east of the Gullard house. But you couldn't be too sure of it, because the snow was drifting and sifting and running like a white river over the ground.

Somewhere off to the left a coyote barked. I turned and looked back toward the house, but it was out of sight. The snow and sleet were slanting at us in streaks that needled the cheeks and nose. Shep was already white, except where my hand grabbed his fur. His ears would point first this way, then that, to try to pick up the barking of the coyote, but he was looking up into my face—to see if I was all right, I guess. All at once I knew what a watch-eye meant. It meant a dog with a watch-eye was the kind of a dog who would watch out for you.

When we moved off again the old buffalo trail—if that's what it was—was gone. Even Shep couldn't find it again, so we let the blizzard blow us, hoping it would keep coming at us out of the north. But within the big storm there were little gales and gusts and eddies that could rattle even a watchdog like Shep. Everybody had heard stories about trappers or hunters who had lost their way in a storm and gone round and round in circles.

But we kept going—there was no turning around and following our footprints home, even if we'd wanted to, because footprints filled up as soon as we took the next step.

Then something white grew out of the gray black ahead—it was a fence post. I let go of Shep and ran to it and touched it. Papa and Jim had cut the cedars that had made the posts, had dug the postholes, and had strung the barbed wires that were now white and singing in the wind.

But we had missed the gate. Which way was it? Right or left? Shep trotted about and sniffed and then looked up at me to ask the same question.

It was while we stood there staring at each other that we heard another sound. Not a coyote this time, but the lower-pitched, pulsating howl of the timber wolf. Shep moved close to me and I reached for him. The hair on his back was standing up and he was growling and whimpering and it scared me because he was scared. "Nothing will come near you as long as you keep moving and swing your lantern," Mamma had said. And by nothing I guess she meant a wolf.

I lifted the lantern and swung it back and forth, and we hurried along the fence. I didn't know whether we were going the right way or the wrong way, but it was away from the ululation of the wolf. Within a minute we came to a break in the wire. The gate! And running through it was the faint depression of the old trail.

I had to let go of Shep to crawl between the second and third wires—the snow was up over the first—and my mackinaw must have caught on a barb. The lantern tipped over. Before I could scramble to my feet, the flame was doused.

I don't know how long I stood there staring at the black lantern. Staring did no good. I tried to let go of it, realizing the lantern would only slow us down from here on, but it would not drop. The handle was frozen to my mitten. With the other hand I felt for Shep. He was right there between me and the sound of the wolf. I found the familiar spot at the nape of his neck and took a firm grip.

Don't think about the wolf, I thought. If you think about something else, you won't even hear it. Think about Mamma and how sick she is and there at home all alone and me so mean and ugly to her all day. "You're not my mother," I had said. I wanted to die. No, don't think about that. Think about what I'm supposed to tell the Gullards when we get there, because we *are* going to get there. Why, isn't that the house up there ahead? No? . . . well, it's got to show up pretty soon, and please, God, don't let us miss it.

The Gullards . . . what am I supposed to tell the Gullards? . . . *Mamma is awful sick—somebody's got to go to Robinson's store and telephone Papa at the Commercial Hotel, then ride on to Aunt Edie and Uncle Corve's and tell them* ... tell them what?

My Time Has Come.

That meant something, didn't it? What? Where had I heard it? Who had said it? About what? . . . *Papa*. Papa had said it. When Uncle Jim died. What was it he said? "When your time comes, you better be packed and ready to go, because the train don't wait for no man!"

I stopped dead still, my hand glued by the snow to Shep's back. I could not breathe or move, and of course I could not see. I could only feel the ice creeping through my clothes.

Mamma was going to die! And she knew it. So you knew it when you were going to die.

I started to run, and Shep began to run even faster, dragging me along.

And then right in front of us was a big black blot, blacker than the black of the blizzard night. I felt my way along the blot, felt the logs of the addition to the Gullard house where the girls slept, felt the washtubs and the clothes boiler that hung on the outside wall, and finally felt the door. I tried to beat on it with my fist, but couldn't make a sound, and then I hauled off and slammed the lantern against the door over and over, and Shep began to howl his fool head off.

A lighted window leapt out of the dark, and then the door opened, and Carl Gullard stood there in his nightgown, looking at me and Shep, and I screamed, "Mamma's going to die! You got to do something!"

"Get in here!" Carl said, and grabbed hold of me and hauled me inside with Shep.

Then Selma and Manda appeared, blinking at the light, rubbing their eyes, their hair in braids for the night, and finally old Chris, pulling his pants up over his nightgown, straightening his mustache, and muttering, "Vat da hell?"

I was crying, I guess, and Carl was trying to get my hand loose from the lantern handle. "He says his ma's going to die," Carl told his father, and old Chris grumbled at the girls about standing around when they ought to be stirring up the fire. Then he reached behind the clock and found a bottle of something and poured a little of it into a glass and held it up to my mouth and said, "Swallow."

I swallowed. Flames licked all the way down to my feet and water shot out of my eyes, and then I strangled and gasped for breath. Old Chris pounded me on the back and then picked me up and set me on his knee, and when I could finally breathe again, he said, "Now then. Tell."

I repeated what Mamma had said I should tell them, and when I was finished old Chris shook his head and said, "Good gosh, boy. Don't you know vat's in de vind?"

I didn't know what he was talking about.

"If dat don't beat the Dutch," he said.

He forgot about me then and told Carl—Harry wasn't home—to get a move on, saddle up and ride down to Robinson's store and telephone Papa and then go on over to the Ransimers' place and roust them out. Meanwhile I was trying to explain why I knew Mamma was going to die, about "My time has come" and all, but nobody was paying any attention. Old Chris was telling Manda to get dressed and come along with him. He could handle it alone if worst came to the worst, he said. God knows he'd had enough practice, he muttered, a couple times without a doctor even, but Jessie might feel easier having a female around, even if the female was just a sprout of sixteen. Till right at the last, that was. Then a woman didn't give two hoots in hell whether she had a man, woman, child, or chimpanzee with her, so long as she had somebody. By that time, God willing, Bob Eunson would be home with the doc.

I wanted to go along with old Chris and Manda, but they wouldn't let me. "Somebody's got to stay here with Selma," Manda said.

That was a lie, and I knew it. Selma was thirteen. She wouldn't be scared to stay alone. They just didn't want me around "right at the last."

But there was nothing I could do. Besides, I felt drowsy. After the rest of them had taken off, I asked Selma what we were going to do about Shep, and she said he'd better stay in the house. If we put him out in the woodshed he and Buster would fight, and a dogfight was all we needed.

She pulled back the covers on Carl's bed, and I got into it, clothes and all, everything but my shoes, and sank out of sight. It was a featherbed, and it felt like a warm, fleecy summer cloud. I had never slept between feathers before, and I wondered why everybody in the world didn't have featherbeds?

I knew I ought to be crying. When your mother dies, you cry. I was sleepy and warm and fuzzy, and sinking, sinking, in the feathery cloud. I tried to cry, but I couldn't.

The old clock in front of the whiskey bottle struck three.

"BUT THAT'S PAPA'S NAME!"

Twenty-Seven

I guess it was around noon when I woke up. Papa was sitting on the side of the bed looking down at me. I didn't know where I was for a minute and then I saw Carl puttering around, pouring himself a cup of coffee, and I remembered, and I could hear Mamma saying, "My time has come."

I was afraid to ask whether her time had really come, but Papa was grinning. If she was dead he sure wouldn't be grinning, would he?

"Upsadaisy," Papa said. "We're going home."

"Is Mamma . . . there?" I asked.

"You bet your sweet life she's there!" he said. "And she's got a surprise for you."

He had come over on Fly, so the two of us rode her home. The storm was over and the sun had come out so bright you had to squint your eyes. If you didn't, you might go snowblind, people said.

Shep trotted along beside us and I told Papa how he'd stuck right with me last night, even when we heard a wolf, and that I'd probably never have made it without him, after the lantern went out, that is. Oh, I might have, but I figured if I laid it on thick, maybe Shep wouldn't have to go back to Billings.

"Who'd you give Shep to?" I finally asked.

"The Smiths," Papa said. "The folks Genevieve boards with. They'd have give him a good home."

"I expect they wouldn't want to keep a dog that chews up his rope and runs away," I said. "You couldn't depend on a dog that'd do a thing like that."

"They won't have a chance to find out," Papa said.

"Why? Aren't you going to give him back to 'em?"

"Jeezlum God!" Papa said. "You don't think I'd give that damn dog away after what he done last night, do you?"

"You mean we're going to keep him?"

"That's what I mean."

"But what if he keeps on killing the Newcomb chickens?"

"I'll pay for every damn last one of 'em!" Papa said. "And if he wants more, I'll buy him a flock all his own!"

Neither one of us said anything for quite a while after that. Then I asked if Aunt Edie and Uncle Corve had come over and Papa said they had. Uncle Corve had gone back home this morning, though. Aunt Edie was going to stay for a few days until things settled down.

"Until what settles down?" I asked.

"You'll see. Everything's going to be different now."

Niles Newcomb was standing outside the house waiting for us and Shep ran up and jumped all over him. It made me sick. You'd think a smart dog like Shep would know it was Mr. Newcomb who had complained about him, but oh, no, not Shep.

Mr. Newcomb said, "Congratulations, Bob," and Papa said, "Thanks, Niles," and then Mr. Newcomb said he was sorry as the devil he'd done what he'd done about our dog, because it seemed like he'd pulled a boner. When he found the dead chickens in his coop and saw our mutt in the vicinity, why, he'd naturally put two and two together and figured it was Shep done it. But this morning he'd gone down to his coop and caught a couple of foxes red-handed. One of 'em had the gall to carry a rooster out with him through the hole they'd made, right while he was watching. "Them same foxes could've got the chickens the first time," Mr. Newcomb said.

"Shep sure didn't get 'em yesterday," Papa said. "He was in Billings with me."

"I guess apologies are in order," Mr. Newcomb said. "No hard feelings?"

"Hell, no," Papa said. "Not on a day like this." Then he turned to me. "What are you sticking around here for? Go on in and take a look at your mamma's surprise."

Everything in the front room was a mess. The dishes hadn't been washed, the boiler was on the stove, and the rack was hung full of wet clothes. That was Aunt Edie for you. Ask her over to call on you, and she'd do the wash.

I walked into the bedroom. Aunt Edie was sitting there beside the bed and Mamma was in it. They were smiling at me and not saying anything, as if they expected me to do something or say something.

I finally said, "I'm sure glad your time didn't come, Mamma."

"But it did," she said. "Come here and look."

I walked over to the bed and she drew back the blankets. Some kind of an animal was in bed with her. It was wiggling and mewling like a kitten, and it was bald and its face and hands—yes, it seemed to have hands and they were doubled up into fists—its face and hands were red.

"What is it?" I asked. I knew, but I couldn't believe it yet.

"It's a baby, what do you think?" Aunt Edie said.

I swallowed hard. "What's its name?"

"Robert," Mamma said. "But that's Papa's name."

"That's right," Aunt Edie said. "He's named for your father."

"We'll call him Bobbie," Mamma said, "while he's little."

I looked at the thing again. "Did you know it was coming?" I asked.

Aunt Edie and Mamma both laughed. "We had a faint idea," Aunt Edie said. Then Mamma pulled up the blanket. "We've got to keep him warm," she said.

"Why didn't you let me in on it?"

"We wanted to surprise you," Mamma said.

"Is *that* the surprise?" I asked, pointing at the baby.

"Of course," Mamma said. "Are you disappointed?"

No, I wasn't disappointed. I was horrified and stunned and furious with myself for being taken in. Here I had spent two years on a farm. I had seen cows and horses swell up and sicken and then deliver their young, and it had never once occurred to me that Mamma's growing fat and short of breath and temper would result in her giving birth to a baby. I must be the stupidest idiot that ever came down the pike!

I turned and ran out of the bedroom, then out of the house. Papa was standing there waiting for me.

"Well," he said, "were you surprised?"

I didn't answer him but kept right on running until I got the sideache and had to flop down or yell. I lay there on my face for a long time, getting my breath. After a while the ache began to ease up. Then I moved my hands and arms and made a butterfly in the snow, and then I felt Shep's nose nuzzling me and sat up.

Our buildings were down there in the foreground, but you had to squint against the sun and snow to see them. Smoke spiraled up out of the stovepipe and reached for the sky today, because the wind had died down. There were the barn and chicken coop and corral, the corncrib I had helped to build, the backhouse, the empty bunkhouse that would house some other hired man, not Jim, come summer.

And beyond all that swept the great plains—to Comanche and Broadview and the Absarokas and the Crazies and the Rockies—and beyond the beyond the Land of Oz—and somewhere beyond even that must be the Sierras and the Pacific, at least that's what it said in your geography book. I tried to think about all that so I would not have to think about what was down there inside the house.

But I could not keep my eyes away from it. A brown puff of smoke rose from the stovepipe. Papa must have put an armload of pitchy wood on the fire. "We've got to keep him warm," Mamma had said.

Him.

Him, not it. He probably wouldn't always be ugly like

that, would he? Someday he'd walk . . . and run . . . and retrieve . . . why, Shep and me might even be able to play with him, if they'd let us.

I stroked Shep's head, and he looked cattercornered out of his watch-eye and licked my face. I said, "Well, whaddaya know, Shep? I got me a brother." It was the first time I'd said it out loud, and it sounded better than I thought it would. Not real yet, but better. *Brother* . . . Harry and Carl were brothers, and they liked each other . . . Papa and Uncle Jim had been brothers, and Papa cried when Uncle Jim died.

Shep just looked at me. He didn't seem to know what I was saying or thinking and I didn't know what was on his mind, if anything. Maybe Mrs. Schultz had finally got in her licks with God.

I got up and tried to make a snowball to throw for Shep but the snow wouldn't stick together. Then Shep noticed something out of the corner of his eye and scooted off after a jackrabbit. He never could catch a full-grown one, but he could sure as hell give it a good workout!

I watched him for a minute or so and then turned and looked down toward the house again. I wanted to go back to it. After a little while I did.

ABOUT THE AUTHOR

Dale Eunson was a successful and prolific writer. In his obituary, the *Los Angeles Times* said Eunson "for seven decades successfully wrote nearly anything that fit on paper—short stories, novels, plays, motion picture scripts and teleplays."

Eunson was born in Wisconsin in 1904. One of his most popular books, *The Day They Gave Babies Away* (1946), is based on his father's true story of trudging through the Wisconsin snows on Christmas Eve of 1868 to find good homes for his five younger siblings after their parents died. Eunson also wrote the novel *Homestead* in 1934, *Up on the Rim* in 1970, and the novel *Philip's Chair* in 1989.

Eunson began writing after his family moved from Montana to California in the early 1920s. After working as a publicist for movie studios, he wrote numerous screenplays, television scripts, Broadway plays, and short stories. His movie credits include the 1950s movie *On the Loose*, starring his daughter, Joan Evans, and *The Star*, featuring Bette Davis. He also wrote for the television shows "Leave It to Beaver" and "Little House on the Prairie." Eunson died in 2002. He was 97.

Western History Classics
Timeless books — great reading

Tenting To-Night   *$19.95, ISBN 1-931832-13-7*
Mary Roberts Rinehart
A family's humorous and lively camping adventure through Montana's Glacier National Park and Washington's North Cascades in 1916.

Blackfeet Tales of Glacier National Park   *$19.95, ISBN 1-931832-14-5*
James Willard Schultz
Introduction by Darrell R. Kipp
20 stories, legends and tales by a man who lived with the Blackfeet Indians in the late 1800s and early 1900s.

Up on the Rim   *$14.95, ISBN 1-931832-20-x*
Dale Eunson
A man's memory of his boyhood days in Montana. Deftly paints an unforgettable picture of homesteading in the early 1900s. Extremely well written. A bookseller's perennial favorite.

War of the Copper Kings   *$19.95, ISBN 1-931832-21-8*
C. B. Glasscock
The best account of Butte's "Copper Kings"—Marcus Daly, W.A. Clark, and F. Augustus Heinze—as they battled for control of "the richest hill on earth."

The Story of Mary MacLane   *$12.95, ISBN 1-931832-19-6*
Mary MacLane
Introduction by Julia Watson
Mary MacLane became an overnight sensation when this book was published in 1902. She was 19 years old and lived in the rough-and-tumble mining town of Butte, Montana. This, her first book, is a breath-taking tour de' force about life, love and longing as fascinating today as it was shocking when first published.

Please look for these books in your local bookstore, or contact
Riverbend Publishing by calling toll-free
1-866-RVR-BEND (787-2363) or write:
Riverbend Publishing
P.O. Box 5833
Helena, MT 59604.
Visit our website at www.riverbendpublishing.com.